LAU...
TRIDUUM MISSAL

with *Palm Sunday & Easter Sunday*

Illustrations by Daniel Mitsui

Laudamus press

P. O. BOX 251, HAMLIN PA 18427
www.laudamus-te.com
contact@laudamus-te.com

Copyright © Laudamus Press 2014
All rights reserved

Cover and book design by Ted Schluenderfritz
Cover image: *Tree of Life* by Pacino Di Bonaguida; photo
courtesy of Galleria dell'Accademia, Florence, Italy
Illustrations by Daniel Mitsui
Text prepared by Margot Davidson
Production by Malcolm Schluenderfritz

All Latin liturgical texts taken from the
1962 edition of *Missale Romanum.*
Special thanks to Alex Begin, Ontario, Canada and Maternal
Heart of Mary Traditional Mass Chaplaincy, Lewisham,
Sydney, Australia for translations of the Mass Propers.
All chants taken from the *Liber Usualis.*

LAUDAMUS PRESS

P. O. Box 251, Hamlin PA 18427
www.laudamus-te.com ✠ *contact@laudamus-te.com*

TABLE OF CONTENTS

The Ordinary of the Mass

The Propers

Chants for the Season

Latin-English
THE ORDINARY OF THE MASS
of the Roman Rite, 1962

The Asperges

The Celebrant begins by intoning the Asperges, the rite in which he sprinkles the Altar, the clergy, and the faithful with holy water. The choir takes up the antiphon while the Celebrant and altar servers recite the concluding prayers. STAND

ANTIPHON *Psalm 50: 9, 3*

ASPERGES ME, *Domine, hyssopo, et mundabor: lavabis me, et super nivem dealbabor. Miserere mei, Deus, secundum magnam misericordiam tuam.* ℣. *Gloria Patri, et Filio, et Spiritui Sancto.* ℟. *Sicut erat in principio, et nunc, et semper, et in sæcula sæculorum. Amen. Ant. Asperges me.*

THOU SHALT SPRINKLE ME, O Lord, with hyssop, and I shall be cleansed; Thou shalt wash me, and I shall become whiter than snow. Have mercy on me, O God, according to Thy great mercy. ℣. Glory be to the Father, and to the Son, and to the Holy Ghost. ℟. As it was in the beginning is now, and ever shall be, world without end. Amen. *Ant.* Thou shalt sprinkle me.

℣. *Ostende nobis, Domine, misericordiam tuam.*
℟. *Et salutare tuum da nobis.*
℣. *Domine, exaudi orationem meam.*
℟. *Et clamor meus ad te veniat.*
℣. *Dominus vobiscum.*
℟. *Et cum spiritu tuo.*
℣. *Oremus.*

℣. Show us, O Lord, Thy mercy.
℟. And grant us Thy salvation.
℣. O Lord, hear my prayer.
℟. And let my cry come unto Thee.
℣. The Lord be with you.
℟. And with thy spirit.
℣. Let us pray.

EXAUDI NOS, *Domine, sancte Pater omnipotens, æterne Deus, et mittere digneris sanctum Angelum tuum de cælis, qui custodiat, foveat, protegat, visitet atque defendat omnes habitantes in hoc habitaculo. Per Christum Dominum nostrum.* ℟. *Amen.*

HEAR US, O Lord, holy Father, almighty and eternal God; and vouchsafe to send Thy holy Angel from heaven to guard, cherish, protect, visit, and defend all that dwell in this house. Through Christ our Lord. ℟. Amen.

MASS OF THE CATECHUMENS

KNEEL *Prayers at the Foot of the Altar*

At Low Mass the faithful kneel until the Gospel. The Celebrant begins by making the Sign of the Cross. Unless otherwise noted, responses are made by the altar servers.

I N THE NAME OF THE FATHER ✠ and of the Son, and of the Holy Ghost. Amen.

℣. I will go in unto the Altar of God.

℟. To God, Who giveth joy to my youth.

IN NOMINE PATRIS ✠ et Filii et Spiritus Sancti. Amen.

℣. *Introibo ad altare Dei.*

℟. *Ad Deum qui lætificat juventutem meam.*

JUDICA ME *Psalm 42*

J UDGE ME, O God, and distinguish my cause from the nation that is not holy: deliver me from the unjust and deceitful man.

℟. For Thou, O God, art my strength: why hast Thou cast me off, and why do I go sorrowful whilst the enemy afflicteth me?

℣. Send forth Thy light and Thy truth: they have led me, and brought me unto Thy holy hill, and into Thy tabernacles.

℟. And I will go in unto the Altar of God: unto God, Who giveth joy to my youth.

℣. I will praise Thee upon the harp, O God, my God: why art thou sad, O my soul, and why dost thou disquiet me?

℟. Hope thou in God, for I will yet praise Him: Who is the salvation of my countenance, and my God.

℣. *JUDICA ME, Deus, et discerne causam meam de gente non sancta; ab homine iniquo et doloso erue me.*

℟. *Quia tu es, Deus, fortitudo mea: quare me repulisti, et quare tristis incedo, dum affligit me inimicus?*

℣. *Emitte lucem tuam et veritatem tuam: ipsa me deduxerunt et adduxerunt in montem sanctum tuum, et in tabernacula tua.*

℟. *Et introibo ad altare Dei: ad Deum qui lætificat juventutem meam.*

℣. *Confitebor tibi in cithara, Deus, Deus meus: quare tristis es, anima mea, et quare conturbas me?*

℟. *Spera in Deo, quoniam adhuc confitebor illi: salutare vultus mei, et Deus meus.*

℣. *Gloria Patri, et Filio, et Spiritui Sancto.*

℟. *Sicut erat in principio, et nunc, et semper, et in sæcula sæculorum. Amen.*

℣. *Introibo ad altare Dei.*

℟. *Ad Deum qui lætificat juventutem meam.*

℣. *Adjutorium nostrum* ✠ *in nomine Domini.*

℟. *Qui fecit cælum et terram.*

℣. Glory be to the Father, and to the Son, and to the Holy Ghost.

℟. As it was in the beginning, is now, and ever shall be, world without end. Amen.

℣. I will go in unto the Altar of God.

℟. To God, Who giveth joy to my youth.

℣. Our help ✠ is in the Name of the Lord.

℟. Who hath made heaven and earth.

The Confiteor

The Celebrant bows to recite the Confiteor.

CONFITEOR DEO OMNIPOTENTI, etc. *[as below]*

I CONFESS TO ALMIGHTY GOD, etc. *[as below]*

℟. *Misereatur tui omnipotens Deus, et dimissis peccatis tuis, perducat te ad vitam æternam.*

℟. May Almighty God have mercy upon thee, forgive thee thy sins, and bring thee to life everlasting.

The Celebrant responds Amen *and stands erect.*

The altar servers recite the Confiteor.

CONFITEOR DEO omnipotenti, *beatæ Mariæ semper Virgini, beato Michæli Archangelo, beato Joanni Baptistæ, sanctis Apostolis Petro et Paulo, omnibus Sanctis, et tibi, pater: quia peccavi nimis cogitatione, verbo et opere; mea culpa, mea culpa, mea maxima culpa. Ideo precor beatam Mariam semper Virginem, beatum Michaelem Archangelum, beatum Joannem Baptistam, sanctos Apostolos Petrum et Paulum, omnes*

I CONFESS TO ALMIGHTY GOD, to blessed Mary ever Virgin, to blessed Michael the Archangel, to blessed John the Baptist, to the holy Apostles Peter and Paul, to all the Saints, and to thee, Father, that I have sinned exceedingly, in thought, word, and deed *Here strike the breast three times* through my fault, through my fault, through my most grievous fault. Therefore I beseech blessed Mary ever Virgin, blessed Michael the Archangel, blessed John the Baptist, the holy Apostles Peter and Paul, all the Saints, and Thee, Father, to pray to the Lord our God for me.

Sanctos, et te, Pater, orare pro me ad Dominum Deum nostrum.

℣. May Almighty God have mercy upon you, forgive you your sins, and bring you to life everlasting.

℟. Amen.

℣. *Misereatur vestri omnipotens Deus, et dimissis peccatis vestris, perducat vos ad vitam æternam.*

℟. *Amen.*

℣. May the Almighty and merciful Lord grant us pardon, ✠ absolution, and remission of our sins.

℟. Amen.

℣. *Indulgentiam ✠ absolutionem et remissionem peccatorum nostrorum tribuat nobis omnipotens et misericors Dominus. ℟. Amen.*

℣. Thou wilt turn, O God, and bring us to life.

℟. And Thy people shall rejoice in Thee.

℣. *Deus, tu conversus vivificabis nos.*

℟. *Et plebs tua lætabitur in te.*

℣. Show us, O Lord, Thy mercy.

℟. And grant us Thy salvation.

℣. *Ostende nobis, Domine, misecordiam tuam.*

℟. *Et salutare tuum da nobis.*

℣. O Lord, hear my prayer.

℟. And let my cry come unto Thee.

℣. *Domine, exaudi orationem meam.*

℟. *Et clamor meus ad te veniat.*

℣. The Lord be with you.

℟. And with thy spirit.

℣. *Dominus vobiscum.*

℟. *Et cum spiritu tuo.*

℣. Let us pray.

℣. *Oremus.*

STAND AT HIGH MASS *Ascending the Altar the Celebrant continues silently.*

TAKE AWAY FROM US our iniquities, we entreat Thee, O Lord, that with pure minds we may worthily enter into the Holy of Holies. Through Christ our Lord. Amen.

AUFER A NOBIS, *quæsumus, Domine, iniquitates nostras, ut ad Sancta Sanctorum puris mereamur mentibus introire. Per Christum Dominum nostrum. Amen.*

He kisses the place where the relics of the saints are enclosed in the Altar, praying silently.

WE BESEECH THEE, O Lord, by the merits of Thy Saints, whose relics are here, and of all the Saints, that Thou

ORAMUS TE, *Domine, per merita sanctorum tuorum, quorum reliquiæ hic sunt, et omnium Sanctorum, ut indulgere digneris omnia peccata mea. Amen.*

wilt deign to pardon me all my sins. Amen.

During a Sung Mass the Celebrant incenses the Altar, blessing the incense by praying.

AB ILLO ✠ BENEDICARIS, *in cujus honore cremaberis. Amen.*

BE ✠ BLESSED BY HIM in whose honour thou art burnt. Amen.

The Introit *see Propers*

The Celebrant makes the Sign of the Cross and recites the Introit antiphon.

The Kyrie Eleison

The choir and faithful chant the Kyrie.

℣. *Kyrie, eleison.*
℟. *Kyrie, eleison.*
℣. *Kyrie, eleison.*
℟. *Christe, eleison.*
℣. *Christe, eleison.*
℟. *Christe, eleison.*
℣. *Kyrie, eleison.*
℟. *Kyrie, eleison.*
℣. *Kyrie, eleison.*

℣. Lord, have mercy on us.
℟. Lord, have mercy on us.
℣. Lord, have mercy on us.
℟. Christ, have mercy on us.
℣. Christ, have mercy on us.
℟. Christ, have mercy on us.
℣. Lord, have mercy on us.
℟. Lord, have mercy on us.
℣. Lord, have mercy on us.

The Gloria

STAND AT HIGH MASS

At High Mass the faithful stand when the Celebrant stands and sit when he sits.

GLORIA IN EXCELSIS DEO, *et in terra pax hominibus bonæ voluntatis. Laudamus te. Benedicimus te. Adoramus te. Glorificamus te. Gratias agimus tibi propter magnam gloriam tuam. Domine Deus, Rex cælestis, Deus Pater omnipotens. Domine Fili unigenite, Jesu Christe, Domine Deus, Agnus Dei, Filius Patris. Qui tollis peccata mundi, miserere nobis. Qui tollis peccata mundi, suscipe deprecationem*

GLORY BE TO GOD ON HIGH. And on earth peace to men of good will. We praise Thee. We bless Thee. We adore Thee. We glorify Thee. We give Thee thanks for Thy great glory. Lord God, heavenly King, God the Father Almighty. Lord Jesus Christ, Only-begotten Son, Lord God, Lamb of God, Son of the Father. Thou Who takest away the sins of the world, have mercy on us. Thou Who takest away the sins of the world receive our prayer.

Thou Who sittest at the right hand of the Father, have mercy on us. For Thou alone art holy. Thou alone art the Lord. Thou alone, O Jesus Christ, art most high. ✠ With the Holy Ghost in the glory of God the Father. Amen.

℣. The Lord be with you.
℟. And with thy spirit.

nostram. Qui sedes ad dexteram Patris, miserere nobis. Quoniam tu solus Sanctus. Tu solus Dominus. Tu solus Altissimus, Jesu Christe. ✠ Cum Sancto Spiritu, in gloria Dei Patris. Amen.

℣. Dominus vobiscum.
℟. Et cum spiritu tuo.

The Collect see Propers
The Celebrant chants the Collect.

SIT
The Epistle see Propers
The Celebrant chants the Epistle.

The Gradual and The Alleluia see Propers
The choir chants the Gradual and Alleluia antiphons that are recited silently by the Celebrant. The Missal is placed on the left side of the Altar, also known as the 'Gospel side'. The incense is blessed, and where a deacon is present he prays the Munda cor meum; *if there is no deacon this prayer is offered by the Celebrant.*

STAND
The Gospel

CLEANSE MY HEART AND MY LIPS, O almighty God, Who didst cleanse the lips of the prophet Isaiah with a burning coal; through Thy gracious mercy so purify me that I may worthily proclaim Thy holy Gospel. Through Christ our Lord. Amen.

PRAY, O Lord, a blessing.

MAY THE LORD be in thy heart and on thy lips that thou mayest worthily and fittingly proclaim His Gospel. In the Name of the Father ✠ and of the Son and of the Holy Ghost. Amen.

MUNDA COR MEUM AC LABIA MEA, omnipotens Deus, qui labia Isaiæ Prophetæ calculo mundasti ignito ita me tua grata miseratione dignare mundare, ut sanctum Evangelium tuum digne valeam nuntiare. Per Christum Dominum nostrum. Amen.

JUBE, Domine, benedicere.

DOMINUS SIT in corde tuo, et in labiis tuis, ut digne et competenter annunties Evangelium suum. In nomine Patris ✠ et Filii, et Spiritus Sancti. Amen.

Stand for the Gospel and make the Sign of the Cross on forehead, lips, and heart.

℣. Dominus vobiscum.

℣. The Lord be with you.

℟. Et cum spiritu tuo.

℟. And with thy spirit.

℣. ✠ Sequentia Sancti Evangelii secundum N.

℣. ✠ The continuation of the holy Gospel according to N.

℟. Gloria tibi, Domine.

℟. Glory to Thee, O Lord.

At the conclusion of the Gospel the Celebrant kisses the book and prays.

℣. Per evangelica dicta, deleantur nostra delicta.

℣. Through the words of the Gospel, may our sins be blotted out.

℟. Laus tibi, Christe.

℟. Praise be to Thee, O Christ.

SIT FOR THE SERMON

The Credo

STAND

CREDO IN UNUM DEUM, *Patrem omnipotentem, factorem cæli et terræ, visibilium omnium et invisibilium. Et in unum Dominum Jesum Christum, Filium Dei unigenitum. Et ex Patre natum ante omnia sæcula, Deum de Deo, lumen de lumine, Deum verum de Deo vero. Genitum, non factum, consubstantialem Patri; per quem omnia facta sunt. Qui propter nos homines, et propter nostram salutem descendit de cælis. Et incarnatus est de Spiritu Sancto ex Maria Virgine et homo factus est. Crucifixus etiam pro nobis, sub Pontio Pilato passus, et sepultus est. Et resurrexit tertia die, secundum Scripturas. Et ascendit in cælum, sedet ad dexteram Patris. Et iterum venturus est cum gloria judicare vivos et mortuos, cujus regni non erit finis. Et in Spiritum Sanctum, Dominum et vivificantem:*

BELIEVE IN ONE GOD, the Father almighty, maker of heaven and earth, and of all things visible and invisible. And in one Lord Jesus Christ, the only-begotten Son of God. Born of the Father before all ages, God of God, Light of Light, true God of true God. Begotten, not made; of one substance with the Father; by Whom all things were made. Who for us men, and for our salvation came down from heaven. GENUFLECT AND BECAME INCARNATE BY THE HOLY GHOST OF THE VIRGIN MARY, AND WAS MADE MAN. He was also crucified for us, suffered under Pontius Pilate, and was buried. And on the third day He rose again according to the Scriptures. He ascended into heaven and sitteth at the right hand of the Father. He will come again in glory to judge the living and the dead and His kingdom will have no end. And in the Holy Ghost, the Lord and Giver of life, Who proceedeth from the Father and the Son. Who together with the Father and the Son is adored and glorified; and Who spoke through the Prophets. And One, Holy, Catholic and Apostolic Church. I confess one baptism for the forgiveness of sins. And I await the resurrection of the dead ✠ and the life of the world to come. Amen.

qui ex Patre, Filioque procedit. Qui cum Patre et Filio simul adoratur et conglorificatur, qui locutus est per Prophetas. Et unam, sanctam, catholicam et apostolicam Ecclesiam. Confiteor unum baptisma in remissionem peccatorum. Et exspecto resurrectionem ✠ mortuorum. Et vitam venturi sæculi. Amen.

MASS OF THE FAITHFUL

STAND *The Celebrant prays aloud and the faithful respond.*

℣. The Lord be with you.
℟. And with thy spirit.

℣. *Dominus vobiscum.*
℟. *Et cum spiritu tuo.*

SIT *The Offertory* see Propers

The choir chants the Offertory antiphon that is recited silently by the Celebrant. He will continue to pray silently until the Preface. Taking the paten, the Celebrant offers up the Host.

ACCEPT, O Holy Father, almighty and eternal God, this unspotted Host, which I, Thine unworthy servant, offer unto Thee, my living and true God, to atone for my countless sins, offenses and negligences, on behalf of all here present and likewise for all faithful Christians, living and dead, that it may avail both me and them as a means of salvation, unto life eternal. Amen.

SUSCIPE, Sancte Pater, omnipotens æterne Deus, hanc immaculatam hostiam, quam ego indignus famulus tuus offero tibi Deo meo vivo et vero, pro innumerabilibus peccatis, et offensionibus, et negligentiis meis, et pro omnibus circumstantibus, sed et pro omnibus fidelibus christianis vivis atque defunctis, ut mihi et illis proficiat ad salutem in vitam æternam. Amen.

Making the Sign of the Cross with the paten, he places the host upon the corporal, a small white linen cloth reserved for this use. The Celebrant blesses the water before it is mixed with the wine in the chalice.

DEUS ✠ qui humanæ substantiæ dignitatem mirabiliter condidisti, et mirabilius reformasti, da nobis per hujus aquæ et vini mysterium, ejus divinitatis esse consortes, qui humanitatis nostræ fieri dignatus est particeps, Jesus Christus Filius tuus Dominus noster, Qui tecum vivit et regnat in unitate Spiritus Sancti Deus, per omnia sæcula sæculorum. Amen.

O GOD ✠ Who in creating man didst exalt his nature very wonderfully and yet more wonderfully didst establish it anew, by the Mystery signified in the mingling of this water and wine, grant us to have part in the Godhead of Him Who hath deigned to become a partaker of our humanity, Jesus Christ, Thy Son, our Lord, Who liveth and reigneth with Thee in the unity of the Holy Ghost, one God, for ever and ever. Amen.

The Celebrant takes up the chalice and offers it to God.

OFFERIMUS TIBI, Domine, calicem salutaris tuam deprecantes clementiam, ut in conspectu divinæ majestatis tuæ, pro nostra et totius mundi salute, cum odore suavitatis ascendat. Amen.

WE OFFER UNTO THEE, O Lord, the chalice of salvation, entreating Thy mercy that our offering may ascend with a sweet fragrance in the sight of Thy divine Majesty, for our own salvation and for that of the whole world. Amen.

He makes the Sign of the Cross with the chalice and places it upon the corporal, covering it with the pall. He bows.

IN SPIRITU HUMILITAS, et in animo contrito suscipiamur a te, Domine, et sic fiat sacrificum nostrum in conspectu tuo hodie, ut placeat tibi, Domine Deus.

HUMBLED IN SPIRIT and contrite of heart, may we find favour with Thee, O Lord, and may our sacrifice be so offered this day in Thy sight as to be pleasing to Thee, O Lord God.

VENI, Sanctificator omnipotens æterne Deus, et benedic ✠ hoc sacrificum, tuo sancto nomini præparatum.

COME, O Sanctifier, almighty and eternal God, and bless ✠ this sacrifice which is prepared for the glory of Thy holy Name.

The Incensing

The Celebrant now blesses the incense.

MAY THE LORD, by the intercession of blessed Michael the Archangel, who standeth at the right side of the altar of incense, and of all His Elect, vouchsafe to bless ✠ this incense and receive it as an odour of sweetness. Through Jesus Christ our Lord. Amen.

PER INTERCESSIONEM beatæ Michaelis Archangeli, stantis a dextris altaris incensi, et omnium electorum suorum, incensum istud dignetur Dominus bene ✠ dicere, et in odorem suavitatis accipere. Per Christum Dominum nostrum. Amen.

He incenses the bread and wine.

May this incense, which Thou hast blessed, O Lord, ascend to Thee, and may Thy mercy descend upon us.

Incensum istud a te benedictum ascendat ad te, Domine, et descendat super nos misericordia tua.

He incenses the Altar.

Let my prayer, O Lord, be directed as incense in Thy sight: the lifting up of my hands as an evening sacrifice. Set a watch, O Lord, before my mouth, and a door round about my lips. May my heart not incline to evil words, to make excuses for sins.

Dirigatur, Domine, oratio mea, sicut incensum in conpectu tuo, elevatio manuum mearum sacrificium vespertinum. Pone, Domine, custodiam ori meo, et ostium circumstantiæ labiis meis. Ut non declinet cor meum in verbo malitiæ, ad excusandas, excusationes in peccata.

Returning the thurible to his assistant the Celebrant prays.

May the Lord enkindle within us the fire of His love, and the flame of everlasting charity. Amen.

Accendat in nobis Dominus ignem sui amoris, et flammam æternæ caritatis. Amen.

The assistant incenses the Celebrant, followed by the clergy. The faithful stand to receive the incense then resume sitting.

The Lavabo

The Celebrant washes his fingers while reciting Psalm 25: 6-12 silently.

I WILL WASH MY HANDS among the innocent, and I will encompass Thine altar, O Lord. That I may hear

LAVABO inter innocentes manus meas, et circumdabo altare tuum, Domine. Ut audiam vocem laudis, et enarrem universa mirabilia tua. Domine, dilexi decorem domus tuæ, et locum habitationis gloriæ tuæ. Ne perdas cum impiis, Deus, animam meam, et cum viris sanguinum vitam meam. In quorum manibus iniquitates sunt, dextera eorum repleta est muneribus. Ego autem in innocentia mea ingressus sum, redime me, et miserere mei. Pes meus stetit in directo, in ecclesiis benedicam te, Domine. Gloria Patri, et Filio, et Spiritui Sancto. Sicut erat in principio, et nunc, et semper, et in sæcula sæculorum. Amen.

the voice of praise, and tell of all Thy wondrous works. I have loved, O Lord, the beauty of Thy house, and the place where Thy glory dwelleth. Take not away my soul, O God, with the wicked, nor my life with men of blood. In whose hands are iniquities, their right hand is filled with gifts. But as for me, I have walked in my innocence; redeem me, and have mercy on me. My foot hath stood in the right way; in the churches I will bless Thee, O Lord. Glory be to the Father, and to the Son, and to the Holy Ghost. As it was in the beginning, is now, and ever shall be, world without end. Amen.

The Prayer to the Holy Trinity

He bows down before the Altar.

SUSCIPE, *sancta Trinitas, hanc oblationem, quam tibi offerimus ob memoriam passionis, resurrectionis, et ascensionis Jesu Christi Domini nostri, et in honorem beatæ Mariæ semper Virginis, et beati Joannis Baptistæ, et sanctorum Apostolorum Petri et Pauli, et istorum, et omnium Sanctorum. Ut illis proficiat ad honorem, nobis autem ad salutem, et illi pro nobis intercedere dignentur in cælis, quorum memoriam agimus in terris. Per eundem Christum Dominum nostrum. Amen.*

RECEIVE, O Holy Trinity, this oblation which we make to Thee in memory of the Passion, Resurrection, and Ascension of our Lord Jesus Christ; and in honour of blessed Mary ever Virgin, of blessed John the Baptist, the holy Apostles Peter and Paul, of these and of all the Saints. To them let it bring honour, and to us salvation, and may they whom we are commemorating here on earth deign to plead for us in heaven. Through the same Christ our Lord. Amen.

The Orate Fratres

The Celebrant kisses the Altar and turning toward the faithful recites aloud the first two words of this prayer, concluding silently.

Pray, brethren, that my Sacrifice and yours may be acceptable to God the Father Almighty.

℟. May the Lord accept the Sacrifice from thy hands, to the praise and glory of His Name, for our benefit and for that of all His holy Church.

℣. Amen.

℣. ORATE *fratres, ut meum ac vestrum sacrificium acceptabile fiat apud Deum Patrem omnipotentem.*

℟. *Suscipiat Dominus sacrificium de manibus tuis ad laudem et gloriam nominis sui, ad utilitatem quoque nostram, totiusque Ecclesiæ suæ sanctæ.* ℣. *Amen.*

The Secret see Propers

He prays the Secret with outstretched hands, concluding aloud. The faithful respond.

℣. For ever and ever.

℟. Amen.

℣. *Per omnia sæcula sæculorum.*

℟. *Amen.*

STAND AT HIGH MASS The Preface of The Holy Cross

The Celebrant chants aloud and the faithful respond.

℣. The Lord be with you.

℟. And with thy spirit.

℣. Lift up your hearts.

℟. We have lifted them up to the Lord.

℣. Let us give thanks to the Lord our God.

℟. It is meet and just.

℣. *Dominus vobiscum.*

℟. *Et cum spiritu tuo.*

℣. *Sursum corda.*

℟. *Habemus ad Dominum.*

℣. *Gratias agamus Domino Deo nostro.*

℟. *Dignum et justum est.*

He chants the Preface.

IT IS TRULY MEET AND JUST, right and for our salvation, that we should at all times, and in all places, give thanks unto Thee, O holy Lord, Father almighty, everlasting God: Who didst establish the salvation of mankind on the tree of the Cross: that whence

VERE DIGNUM ET IUSTUM EST, *aequum et salutare, nos tibi semper et ubique gratias agere: Domine, sancte Pater, omnipotens aeterne Deus: Qui salutem humani generis in ligno Crucis constituisti: ut unde mors oriebatur, inde vita resurgeret:*

et, qui in ligno vincebat, in ligno quoque vinceretur: per Christum Dominum nostrum. Per quem maiestatem tuam laudant Angeli, adorant Dominationes, tremunt Potestates. Caeli caelorumque Virtutes, ac beata Seraphim, socia exsultatione concelebrant. Cum quibus et nostras voces ut admitti iubeas, deprecamur, supplici confessione dicentes...

death came, thence also life might arise again, and that he who overcame by the tree, by the tree also might be overcome, through Christ our Lord. Through Whom the Angels praise Thy Majesty, the Dominions worship it, the Powers stand in awe. The heavens and the heavenly hosts together with the blessed Seraphim in triumphant chorus unite to celebrate it. Together with these we entreat Thee, that Thou mayest bid our voices also to be admitted while we say with lowly praise...

The Sanctus

KNEEL

The Celebrant intones the Sanctus, in which the choir and faithful join.
🌲🌲🌲 *At Low Mass kneel for the Sanctus and do not rise again until Communion.*

SANCTUS, *sanctus, sanctus. Dominus Deus sabaoth. Pleni sunt caeli et terra gloria tua. Hosanna in excelsis.* ✠ *Benedictus qui venit in nomine Domini. Hosanna in excelsis.*

HOLY, holy, holy Lord God of Hosts. Heaven and earth are full of Thy glory. Hosanna in the highest. ✠ Blessed is He who comes in the Name of the Lord. Hosanna in the highest.

CANON OF THE MASS

Bowing low over the Altar, the Celebrant begins the Canon silently. He will continue silently until he concludes the Final Doxology and Minor Elevation.

Prayers Before the Consecration

FOR THE CHURCH

TE IGITUR, *clementissime Pater, per Jesum Christum Filium tuum, Dominum nostrum, supplices rogamus, ac petimus, uti accepta habeas, et benedicas, hæc* ✠ *dona,*

MOST MERCIFUL FATHER, we humbly pray and beseech Thee, through Jesus Christ Thy Son, our Lord, to accept and bless these ✠ gifts, these ✠ presents, these ✠ holy unspotted Sacrifices, which we offer up to Thee, in the first place, for Thy Holy Catholic Church, that it may please Thee to grant her peace, to preserve, unite, and govern her throughout the world; as also for Thy servant N. our Pope, and N. our bishop, and for all orthodox believers and all who profess the Catholic and Apostolic faith.

hæc ✠ munera, hæc ✠ sancta sacrificia illibata, in primis, quæ tibi offerimus pro Ecclesia tua sancta catholica, quam pacificare, custodire, adunare, et regere digneris toto orbe terrarum, una cum famulo tuo Papa nostro N. et Antistite nostro N. et omnibus orthodoxis atque catholicæ et apostolicæ fidei cultoribus.

FOR THE LIVING

BE MINDFUL, O Lord, of Thy servants and handmaids, N. and N., and of all here present, whose faith and devotion are known to Thee, for whom we offer, or who offer up to Thee, this Sacrifice of praise for themselves and all those dear to them, for the redemption of their souls and the hope of their safety and salvation, who now pay their vows to Thee, the eternal, living and true God.

MEMENTO, Domine, famulorum, famularumque tuarum, N. et N., et omnium circumstantium, quorum tibi fides cognita est, et nota devotio, pro quibus tibi offerimus, vel qui tibi offerunt hoc sacrificium laudis, pro se, suisque omnibus, pro redemptione animarum suarum, pro spe salutis, et incolumitatis suæ: tibique reddunt vota sua æterno Deo, vivo et vero.

INVOCATION OF THE SAINTS
The Communicantes *may change to reflect special feast days.*

IN COMMUNION WITH, and honouring the memory in the first place of the glorious ever Virgin Mary Mother of our God and Lord Jesus Christ; also blessed Joseph, her Spouse; and likewise of Thy blessed Apostles and Martyrs, Peter and Paul, Andrew, James, John, Thomas, James, Philip, Bartholomew, Matthew, Simon and

COMMUNICANTES, et memoriam venerantes, in primis gloriosæ semper Virginis Mariæ, Genitricis Dei et Domini nostri Jesu Christi, sed et beati Joseph ejusdem Virginis Sponsi, et beatorum Apostolorum ac Martyrum tuorum, Petri et Pauli, Andreæ, Jacobi, Joannis, Thomæ, Jacobi, Philippi, Bartholomæi, Matthæi, Simonis et Thaddæi, Lini, Cleti, Clementis, Xysti, Cornelii, Cypriani, Laurentii, Chrysogoni, Joannis et Pauli, Cosmæ et Damiani, et omnium Sanctorum tuorum. Quorum meritis precibusque concedas, ut in omnibus protectionis tuæ muniamur auxilio. Per eundem Christum Dominum nostrum. Amen.

Thaddeus, Linus, Cletus, Clement, Sixtus, Cornelius, Cyprian, Lawrence, Chrysogonus, John and Paul, Cosmas and Damian, and of all Thy Saints. Grant for the sake of their merits and prayers that in all things we may be guarded and helped by Thy protection. Through the same Christ our Lord. Amen.

The Consecration

HANC IGITUR OBLATIONEM servitutis nostræ, sed et cunctæ familiæ tum, quæsumus, Domine, ut placatus accipias. Diesque nostros in tua pace disponas, atque ab acterna damnatione nos eripi, et in electorum tuorum jubeas grege numerari. Per Christum Dominum nostrum. Amen.

WE THEREFORE BESEECH THEE, O Lord, graciously to accept this oblation of our service and that of Thy whole household. Order our days in Thy peace, and command that we be rescued from eternal damnation and numbered in the flock of Thine elect. Through Christ our Lord. Amen.

QUAM OBLATIONEM TU, Deus, in omnibus, quæsumus, bene ✠ dictam, adscrip ✠ tam, ra ✠ tam, rationabilem, acceptabilemque facere digneris, ut nobis Cor ✠ pus, et San ✠ guis fiat dilectissimi Filii tui Domini nostri Jesu Christi.

HUMBLY WE PRAY THEE, O God, be pleased to make this same offering wholly ✠ blessed, to ✠ consecrate it and ✠ approve it, making it reasonable and acceptable, that it may become for us the ✠ Body and ✠ Blood of Thy dearly beloved Son, our Lord Jesus Christ.

WORDS OF CONSECRATION AND ELEVATION

QUI PRIDIE QUAM PATERETUR, accepit panem in sanctas ac venerabiles manus suas, et elevatis oculis in cælum ad te Deum Patrem suum omnipotentem tibi gratias

WHO, the day before He suffered, took bread into His Holy and venerable hands, and having lifted His eyes to heaven, to Thee, God, His Almighty Father, giving thanks to Thee, ✠ blessed it, broke it, and gave it to His disciples, saying: Take and eat ye all of this.

agens, bene ✠ dixit, fregit, deditque discipulis suis, dicens: Accipite, et manducate ex hoc omnes.

FOR THIS IS MY BODY.

HOC EST ENIM CORPUS MEUM.

🔺 🔺 🔺 *The Celebrant genuflects, adores the Sacred Host, and rising elevates It. Placing It on the corporal, he again adores It. Then he uncovers the chalice.*

IN LIKE MANNER, after He had supped, taking also into His holy and venerable hands this goodly chalice, giving thanks to Thee, He ✠ blessed it, and gave it to His disciples, saying: Take and drink ye all of this.

SIMILI MODO POSTQUAM cenatum est, accipiens et hunc præclarum Calicem in sanctas ac venerabiles manus suas, item tibi gratias agens, bene ✠ dixit, deditque discipulis suis, dicens: Accipite, et bibite ex eo omnes.

FOR THIS IS THE CHALICE OF MY BLOOD, of the new and eternal Testament, the mystery of Faith, which shall be shed for you and for many unto the remission of sins.

HIC EST ENIM CALIX SANGUINIS MEI, novi et aeterni testamenti, mysterium fidei, qui pro vobis et pro multis effundetur in remissionem peccatorum.

🔺 🔺 🔺 *The Celebrant genuflects and rising elevates the Chalice. Placing It on the corporal, he covers It and again adores It. He continues silently.*

As often as ye shall do these things, ye shall do them in remembrance of Me.

Hæc quotiescumque feceritis, in mei memoriam facietis.

Prayers After the Consecration
OBLATION OF THE VICTIM TO GOD

AND NOW, O Lord, we, Thy servants, and with us all Thy holy people, calling to mind the blessed Passion of this same Christ, Thy Son, our Lord, likewise His Resurrection from the grave, and also His glorious Ascension into heaven, do offer unto Thy most sovereign Majesty out of the gifts Thou hast bestowed upon us, a Victim which is ✠ pure, a Victim which is

UNDE ET MEMORES, Domine, nos servi tui, sed et plebs tua sancta, ejusdem Christi Filii tui Domini nostri tam beatæ Passionis, nec non et ab inferis Resurrectionis, sed et in cælos gloriosæ ascensionis, offerimus præclaræ majestati tuæ de tuis donis ac datis hostiam pu ✠ ram, hostiam sanc ✠ tam, hostiam immacu ✠ latam, Panem

✠ *sanctum vitæ æternæ, et* ✠ *Calicem salutis perpetuæ.*

✠ holy, a Victim which is ✠ spotless, the ✠ holy Bread of life eternal, and the ✠ Chalice of everlasting Salvation.

SUPRA QUÆ PROPITIO AC serene vultu respicere digneris, et accepta habere, sicuti accepta habere dignatus es munera pueri tui justi Abel, et sacrificium Patriarchæ nostri Abrahæ, et quod tibi obtulit summus sacerdos tuus Melchisedech, sanctum sacrificium, immaculatam hostiam.

DEIGN TO LOOK UPON THEM with a favourable and gracious countenance, and to accept them as Thou didst accept the offerings of Thy just servant Abel, and the sacrifice of our Patriarch Abraham, and that which Thy high priest Melchisedech offered up to Thee, a holy Sacrifice, an immaculate victim.

FOR BLESSINGS

SUPPLICES TE ROGAMUS, omnipotens Deus, jube hæc perferri per manus Sancti Angeli tui in sublime altare tuum, in conspectu divinæ majestatis tuæ, ut quoquot ex hac altaris participatione, sacrosanctum Filii tui Cor ✠ *pus, et San* ✠ *guinem sumpserimus omni benedictione cælesti et gratia repleamur. Per eundem Christum Dominum nostrum. Amen.*

HUMBLY we beseech Thee, almighty God, to command that these our offerings be carried by the hands of Thy holy Angel to Thine Altar on high, in the sight of Thy divine Majesty, so that those of us who shall receive the most sacred ✠ Body and ✠ Blood of Thy Son by partaking thereof from this Altar may be filled with every grace and heavenly blessing. Through Christ our Lord. Amen.

FOR THE DEAD

MEMENTO ETIAM, Domine, famulorum famularumque tuarum, N. et N., qui nos præcesserunt cum signo fidei, et dormiunt in somno pacis. Ipsis, Domine, et omnibus in Christo quiescentibus, locum refrigerii, lucis et pacis, ut indulgeas, deprecamur. Per eundem Christum Dominum nostrum. Amen.

BE MINDFUL, also, O Lord, of Thy servants and handmaids N. and N. who are gone before us with the sign of faith and who sleep the sleep of peace. To these, O Lord, and to all who rest in Christ, grant, we beseech Thee, a place of refreshment, light, and peace. Through the same Christ our Lord. Amen.

FOR THE FAITHFUL

TO US ALSO THY SINFUL SERVANTS, who put our trust in the multitude of Thy mercies, vouchsafe to grant some part and fellowship with Thy Holy Apostles and Martyrs, with John, Stephen, Matthias, Barnabas, Ignatius, Alexander, Marcellinus, Peter, Felicity, Perpetua, Agatha, Lucy, Agnes, Cecilia, Anastasia, and all Thy Saints. Into their company we beseech Thee admit us, not considering our merits, but freely pardoning our offenses. Through Christ our Lord.

NOBIS QUOQUE peccatoribus, famulis tuis, de multitudine miserationum tuarum sperantibus, partem aliquam, et societatem donare digneris, cum tuis sanctis Apostolis et Martyribus, cum Joanne, Stephano, Matthia, Barnaba, Ignacio, Alexandro, Marcellino, Petro, Felicitate, Perpetua, Agatha, Lucia, Agnete, Cæcilia, Anastasia, et omnibus Sanctis tuis. Intra quorum nos consortium, non æstimator meriti, sed veniæ, quæsumus, largitor admitte. Per Christum Dominum nostrum.

THE FINAL DOXOLOGY AND MINOR ELEVATION

THROUGH WHOM, O Lord, Thou dost ✠ create, ✠ sanctify, ✠ quicken, ✠ bless, and bestow upon us all these good things. Through ✠ Him, and with ✠ Him and in ✠ Him, is unto Thee, ✠ God the Father Almighty, in the unity of the ✠ Holy Ghost, all honour and glory.

PER QUEM HÆC OMNIA DOMINE, semper bona creas, sancti ✠ ficas, vivi ✠ ficas, bene ✠ dicis, et præstas nobis. Per ip ✠ sum, et cum ip ✠ so, et in ip ✠ so, est tibi Deo Patri ✠ omnipotenti, in unitate Spiritus ✠ Sancti, omnis honor et gloria.

The Celebrant concludes aloud and the faithful respond.

℣. For ever and ever.
℞. Amen.

℣. *Per omnia sæcula sæculorum.*
℞. *Amen.*

STAND AT HIGH MASS   *The Pater Noster*

He joins his hands and prays.

Let us pray.

Oremus.

Taught by our Saviour's command and formed by divine teaching, we dare to say:

Præceptis salutaribus moniti, et divina institutione formati, audemus dicere:

PATER NOSTER, qui es in cælis, sanctificetur nomen tuum, adveniat regnum tuum, fiat voluntas tua, sicut in cælo, et in terra. Panem nostrum quotidianum da nobis hodie, et dimitte nobis debita nostra, sicut et nos dimittimus debitoribus nostris. Et ne nos inducas in tentationem.

℞. Sed libera nos a malo.

℣. Amen.

The Celebrant continues silently.

LIBERA NOS, quæsumus, Domine, ab omnibus malis, præteritis, præsentibus, et futuris, et intercedente beata et gloriosa semper Virgine Dei Genitrice Maria, cum beatis Apostolis tuis Petro et Paulo, atque Andrea, et omnibus San ✠ ctis, da propitius pacem in diebus nostris, ut, ope misericordiæ tuæ adjuti, et a peccato simus semper liberi, et ab omni perturbatione securi.

He breaks the Host over the Chalice.

Per eumdem Dominum nostrum Jesum Christum, Filium tuum.

He breaks a Particle from the divided Host.

Qui tecum vivit et regnat in unitate Spiritus Sancti Deus.

The Celebrant concludes aloud and the faithful respond.

℣. Per omnia sæcula sæculorum.

℞. Amen.

OUR FATHER, Who art in heaven, hallowed be Thy Name; Thy Kingdom come; Thy will be done on earth as it is in heaven. Give us this day our daily bread; and forgive us our trespasses as we forgive those who trespass against us. And lead us not into temptation.

℞. But deliver us from evil.

℣. AMEN.

DELIVER US, we beseech Thee, O Lord, from all evils, past, present, and to come; and by the intercession of the blessed and glorious Mary, ever Virgin, Mother of God, together with Thy blessed Apostles Peter and Paul, and Andrew, and all the ✠ Saints, mercifully grant us peace in our days, that through the bounteous help of Thy mercy, we may be always free from sin and safe from all disquiet.

Through the same Jesus Christ, Thy Son, our Lord.

Who liveth and reigneth with Thee in the unity of the Holy Ghost, God.

℣. For ever and ever.

℞. Amen.

The Commingling of the Sacred Body and Blood

He makes the Sign of the Cross over the Chalice with the Particle, praying aloud. The faithful respond.

℣. May the peace ✠ of the Lord be ✠ always ✠ with you.

℟. AND WITH THY SPIRIT.

℣. *Pax ✠ Domini sit ✠ semper ✠ vobiscum.*

℟. *Et cum spiritu tuo.*

KNEEL AT HIGH MASS *He continues silently.*

MAY THIS MINGLING and hallowing of the Body and Blood of our Lord Jesus Christ be for us who receive it a source of eternal life. Amen.

HAEC COMMIXTIO, et consecratio Corporis et Sanguinis Domini nostri Jesu Christi, fiat accipientibus nobis in vitam æternam. Amen.

The Agnus Dei

The choir and faithful chant the Agnus Dei that is recited silently by the Celebrant and altar servers.

LAMB OF GOD, Who takest away the sins of the world, have mercy on us.

AGNUS DEI, qui tollis peccata mundi: miserere nobis.

Lamb of God, Who takest away the sins of the world, have mercy on us.

Agnus Dei, qui tollis peccata mundi: miserere nobis.

Lamb of God, Who takest away the sins of the world, grant us peace.

Agnus Dei, qui tollis peccata mundi: dona nobis pacem.

Prayers for Holy Communion

THE PRAYER FOR PEACE

O LORD, JESUS CHRIST, Who didst say to Thine Apostles: Peace I leave you, My peace I give you: look not upon my sins, but upon the faith of Thy Church; and deign to give her that peace and unity which is agreeable to Thy will. God Who livest and reignest world without end. Amen.

DOMINE JESU CHRISTE, qui dixisti Apostolis tuis: Pacem relinquo vobis, pacem meam do vobis: ne respicias peccata mea, sed fidem Ecclesiæ tuæ, eamque secundum voluntatem tuam pacificare et coadunare digneris. Qui vivis et regnas Deus per omnia sæcula sæculorum. Amen.

At a Solemn Mass the Celebrant bestows the kiss of peace upon the Deacon, who in turn bears it to clergy present on the Altar.

℣. *Pax tecum.*

℟. *Et cum spiritu tuo.*

℣. Peace be with thee.

℟. And with thy spirit.

THE PRAYER FOR SANCTIFICATION

DOMINE JESU CHRISTE, Fili Dei vivi, qui ex voluntate Patris, cooperante Spiritu Sancto, per mortem tuam mundum vivificasti, libera me per hoc sacrosanctum Corpus et Sanguinem tuum ab omnibus iniquitatibus meis, et universis malis, et fac me tuis semper inhærere mandatis, et a te numquam separari permittas. Qui cum eodem Deo Patre et Spiritu Sancto vivis et regnas, Deus, in sæcula sæculorum. Amen.

O LORD JESUS CHRIST, Son of the living God, Who, by the will of the Father and the cooperation of the Holy Ghost, has by Thy death given life to the world: deliver me by this, Thy most sacred Body and Blood, from all my iniquities and from every evil; make me cling always to Thy commandments, and permit me never to be separated from Thee. Who with the same God, the Father and the Holy Ghost, livest and reignest God, world without end. Amen.

THE PRAYER FOR GRACE

PERCEPTIO CORPORIS TUI, Domine Jesu Christe, quod ego indignus sumere præsumo, non mihi proveniat in judicium et condemnationem, sed pro tua pietate prosit mihi ad tutamentum mentis et corporis, et ad medelam percipiendam. Qui vivis et regnas cum Deo Patre in unitate Spiritus Sancti, Deus, per omnia sæcula sæculorum. Amen.

LET NOT THE PARTAKING of Thy Body, O Lord Jesus Christ, which I, though unworthy, presume to receive, turn to my judgment and condemnation; but through Thy mercy, may it be unto me a safeguard and a healing remedy both of soul and body. Who livest and reignest with God the Father, in the unity of the Holy Ghost, God, for ever and ever. Amen.

The Prayers at the Communion

PANEM CÆLESTEM ACCIPIAM, et nomen Domini invocabo.

I WILL TAKE the Bread of Heaven, and will call upon the Name of the Lord.

♠ ♠ ♠ *Striking his breast three times, the Celebrant prays three times audibly.*

LORD, I am not worthy that Thou shouldst enter under my roof, but only say the word, and my soul shall be healed.

DOMINE, non sum dignis, ut intres sub tectum meum, sed tantum dic verbo, et sanabitur anima mea.

Then making the Sign of the Cross with the Host over the paten, he continues silently.

MAY THE BODY of Our Lord Jesus Christ preserve my soul unto life everlasting. Amen.

CORPUS DOMINI NOSTRI Jesu Christi custodiat animam meam in vitam æternam. Amen.

The Celebrant receives the Host. He uncovers the Chalice, genuflects, and collects any Fragments remaining and purifies the paten over the Chalice.

WHAT RETURN SHALL I MAKE to the Lord for all the things that He hast given unto me? I will take the chalice of salvation, and call upon the Name of the Lord. I will call upon the Lord and give praise, and I shall be saved from mine enemies.

QUID RETRIBUAM Domino pro omnibus quæ retribuit mihi? Calicem salutaris accipiam, et nomen Domini invocabo. Laudans invocabo Dominum, et ab inimicis meis salvus ero.

He makes the Sign of the Cross with the Chalice.

MAY THE BLOOD of our Lord Jesus Christ preserve my soul unto life everlasting. Amen.

SANGUIS DOMINI nostri Jesu Christi custodiat animam meam in vitam æternam. Amen.

The Celebrant receives the Precious Blood. He genuflects, elevates a Particle of the Host, and turning toward the faithful says aloud.

BEHOLD THE LAMB OF GOD, behold Him who taketh away the sins of the world.

ECCE AGNUS DEI, ecce qui tollit peccata mundi.

The faithful adore the Sacred Host, and striking their breasts three times say three times aloud,

LORD, I am not worthy that Thou shouldst enter under my roof; but only say the word, and my soul shall be healed.

DOMINE, non sum dignis, ut intres sub tectum meum, sed tantum dic verbo, et sanabitur anima mea.

Communicants receive on the tongue while kneeling at the Altar rail unless there is a disability. The Celebrant approaches each, saying,

CORPUS DOMINI nostri Jesu Christi custodiat animam tuam in vitam æternam. Amen.

MAY THE BODY of Our Lord Jesus Christ preserve your soul unto life everlasting. Amen.

The communicant does not respond. Those attending Mass are reminded that only baptized Catholics who are in the state of grace and have observed the fast may receive Holy Communion. Communicants resume kneeling in the pew to make their thanksgiving.

THE PRAYERS DURING THE ABLUTIONS

The Celebrant continues silently.

QUOD ORE SUMPSIMUS, Domine, pura mente capiamus, et de munere temporali fiat nobis remedium sempiternum.

GRANT, O Lord, that what we have taken with our mouth, we may receive with a pure mind; and that from a temporal gift it may become for us an eternal remedy.

Wine and water are poured over the fingers of the Celebrant into the Chalice.

CORPUS TUUM, Domine, quod sumpsi, et Sanguis, quem potavi, adhæreat visceribus meis, et præsta ut in me non remaneat scelerum macula, quem pura et sancta refecerunt sacramenta. Qui vivis et regnas in sæcula sæculorum. Amen.

MAY THY BODY, O LORD, which I have received and Thy Blood which I have drunk, cleave to my inmost parts, and grant that no stain of sin remain in me, whom these pure and holy Sacraments have refreshed. Who livest and reignest for ever and ever. Amen.

The Communion Antiphon see Propers STAND AT HIGH MASS

This prayer is chanted by the choir during communion at a Sung Mass, or by the Celebrant afterward.

The Postcommunion Antiphon see Propers

This prayer is chanted by the choir after communion at a Sung Mass, or by the Celebrant after the Communion Antiphon. He concludes aloud,

℞. Oremus.

℣. Dominus vobiscum.

℞. Et cum spiritu tuo.

℞. Let us pray.

℣. The Lord be with you.

℞. And with thy spirit.

The Dismissal

The Celebrant intones and the faithful respond.

℣. Go, the Mass is ended.

℟. Thanks be to God.

℣. *Ite, Missa est.*

℟. *Deo gratias.*

KNEEL   ## The Blessing

Bowing before the Altar the Celebrant prays silently.

MAY THE TRIBUTE OF MY HOMAGE be pleasing to Thee, O most holy Trinity. Grant that the Sacrifice which I, unworthy as I am, have offered in the presence of Thy Majesty, may be acceptable to Thee. Through Thy mercy may it bring forgiveness to me and to all for whom I have offered it. Through Christ our Lord. Amen.

PLACEAT TIBI, sancta Trinitas, obsequium servitutis meæ. Et præsta ut sacrificium, quod oculis tuæ majestatis indignus obtuli, tibi sit acceptabile, mihique et omnibus, pro quibus illud obtuli, sit, te miserante, propitiabile. Per Christum Dominum nostrum. Amen.

He kisses the Altar then turns toward the faithful, blessing them. The faithful respond.

May almighty God bless you, the Father, the Son ✠ and the Holy Ghost.

℟. Amen.

℣. *Benedicat vos omnipotens Deus, Pater, et ✠ Filius, et Spiritus Sanctus.* ℟. *Amen.*

STAND   ## The Last Gospel John 1: 1-14

The Celebrant begins aloud. The faithful respond, stand for the Gospel, and make the Sign of the Cross on forehead, lips, and heart.

℣. The Lord be with you.

℟. And with thy spirit.

℣. ✠ The beginning of the holy Gospel according to Saint John.

℟. GLORY TO THEE, O LORD.

℣. *Dominus vobiscum.*

℟. *Et cum spiritu tuo.*

℣. ✠ *Initium Sancti Evangelii secundum Joannem.*

℟. *Gloria tibi, Domine.*

He reads the Gospel.

IN THE BEGINNING WAS THE WORD, and the Word was with God, and the Word was God. The same was in the beginning with God. All things were

IN PRINCIPIO ERAT VERBUM, et Verbum erat apud Deum, et Deus erat Verbum. Hoc erat in principio apud Deum. Omnia

per ipsum facta sunt, et sine ipso factum est nihil quod factum est, in ipso vita erat, et vita erat lux hominum. Et lux in tenebris lucet, et tenebræ eam non comprehenderunt. Fuit homo missus a Deo cui nomen erat Joannes. Hic venit in testimonium, ut testimonium perhiberet de lumine, ut omnes crederent per illum. Non erat ille lux, sed ut testimonium perhiberet de lumine. Erat lux vera quæ illuminat omnem hominem venientem in hunc mundum. In mundo erat, et mundus per ipsum factus est, et mundus eum non cognovit. In propria venit, et sui eum non receperunt. Quotquot autem receperunt eum, dedit eis potestatem filios Dei fieri, his, qui credunt in nomine ejus, qui non ex sanguinibus, neque ex voluntate carnis, neque ex voluntate viri, sed ex Deo nati sunt. ET VERBUM CARO FACTUM EST et habitavit in nobis, et vidimus gloriam ejus, gloriam quasi Unigeniti a Patre, plenum gratiæ et veritatis.

℟. *Deo gratias.*

made by Him; and without Him was not any thing made that was made. In Him was life; and the life was the Light of men. And the Light shineth in darkness; and the darkness comprehended it not. There was a man sent from God, whose name was John. The same came for a witness, to bear witness of the Light, that all men through Him might believe. He was not that Light, but was sent to bear witness of that Light. That was the true Light, which lighteth every man that cometh into the world. He was in the world, and the world was made by Him, and the world knew Him not. He came unto His own, and His own received Him not. But as many as received Him, to them He gave power to become the sons of God, even to them that believe in His Name, which were born, not of blood, nor of the will of the flesh, nor of the will of man, but of God. GENUFLECT AND THE WORD WAS MADE FLESH and dwelt among us, and we beheld His glory, the glory as it were of the Only begotten of the Father, full of grace and truth.

℟. Thanks be to God.

✠   ✠   ✠

PRAYERS AFTER MASS

In 1884, Pope Leo XIII prescribed the recitation of prayers after Low Mass. In 1934, Pope Pius XI ordered that these same prayers be offered for the conversion of Russia. The Priest leads the faithful in reciting the Hail Mary three times, then the Hail Holy Queen, the prayer to St. Michael the Archangel, and the invocation of the Sacred Heart of Jesus.

KNEEL   ## Hail Holy Queen

HAIL, HOLY QUEEN, mother of mercy; hail, our life, our sweetness, and our hope! To thee do we cry, poor banished children of Eve; To thee do we send up our sighs, mourning and weeping in this valley of tears. Turn then, most gracious Advocate, thine eyes of mercy towards us; and after this our exile, show unto us the blessed fruit of thy womb, Jesus. O clement, O loving, O sweet Virgin Mary!

℣. Pray for us, O holy Mother of God.
℟. That we may be made worthy of the promises of Christ.
℣. Let us pray.

O GOD, OUR REFUGE and our strength, mercifully look down on Thy people who cry to Thee, and through the intercession of the glorious and immaculate Virgin Mary, Mother of God, of Saint Joseph her Spouse, of Thy blessed Apostles Peter and Paul, and of all the saints, in mercy and goodness hear our prayers for the conversion of sinners, and for the liberty and exultation of our holy Mother the Church. Through the same Christ our Lord. ℟. Amen.

SALVE REGÍNA, mater misericórdiæ; vita, dulcédo, et spes nostra, salve. Ad te clamámus, éxsules fílii Evæ. Ad te suspirámus, geméntes et flentes in hac lacrymárum valle. Eia ergo, Advocáta nostra, illos tuos misericórdes óculos ad nos convérte. Et Jesum, benedíctum fructum ventris tui, nobis post hoc exsílium osténde. O clemens, O pia, O dulcis Virgo María.

℣. *Ora pro nobis, sancta Dei Génitrix.*
℟. *Ut digni efficiámur promissiónibus Christi.*
℣. *Oremus.*

DEUS REFUGIUM NOSTRUM et virtus, populum ad te clamantem propitius respice, et intercedente gloriosa et immaculata Virgine Dei Genitrice Maria, cum beato Josepho ejus Sponso, ac beatis Apostolis tuis Petro et Paulo, et omnibus Sanctis, quas pro conversione peccatorum, pro libertate et exaltatione sanctæ Matris Ecclesiæ, preces effundimus, misericors et benignus exaudi. Per eundem Christum Dominum nostrum.
℟. *Amen.*

Prayer to St. Michael the Archangel

SANCTE MICHAEL ARCHANGELE, defende nos in prælio. Contra nequitiam et insidias diaboli esto præsidium. Imperet illi Deus, supplices deprecamur. Tuque princeps militiæ cælestis, Satanam aliosque spiritus malignos, qui ad perditionem animarum pervagantur in mundo divina virtute in infernum detrude. R̠. Amen.

Saint Michael the Archangel, defend us in battle. Be our protection against the wickedness and snares of the devil. May God rebuke him, we humbly pray; and do Thou, O Prince of the Heavenly Host, by the Divine Power of God, cast into hell satan and all evil spirits who prowl about the world, seeking the ruin of souls. R̠. Amen.

Invocation to the Sacred Heart

He concludes by saying three times, and the faithful respond with each invocation,

V̠. Cor Jesu sacratissimum.
R̠. Miserere nobis.

V̠. Most Sacred Heart of Jesus.
R̠. Have mercy on us.

✠   ✠   ✠

Prayers After Holy Communion

PRAYER OF ST. THOMAS AQUINAS

I GIVE THANKS TO THEE, O holy Lord, Father almighty, eternal God, Who hast vouchsafed, not for any merits of my own but solely out of the condescension of Thy mercy, to appease the hunger of the soul of Thine unworthy servant, with the precious Body and Blood of Thy Son our Lord Jesus Christ. I implore that this holy Communion be not to me a condemnation unto punishment, but a saving plea unto forgiveness. May it be unto me the armor of faith and the shield of good purpose. May it be the emptying out of my vices, the extinction of all concupiscence and lust, the increase of charity and patience, of humility and obedience, and of all virtues; a strong defense against the snares of all enemies, visible and invisible; the perfect quieting of all my impulses, both fleshly and ghostly; a firm cleaving unto Thee, the one true God; and a pledge of a blessed destiny. And I beseech Thee, that Thou wouldst vouchsafe to bring me, a sinner, to that ineffable Banquet, in which Thou, together with Thy Son and the Holy Ghost, art to Thy Saints true light, fullness of content, eternal joy, gladness without alloy, and perfect happiness. Through the same Christ our Lord. Amen.

BLESS THE LORD, O my soul! and let all that is within me bless His holy name. "Bless the Lord, O my soul! and never forget all that He hath done for thee." Let my soul, O Lord, be sensible of its happiness. Let it, in the silence of all worldly cares, taste and enjoy the sweetness of Thy presence. "It is good for me to adhere to my God, to put my hope in the Lord God. I will hear what the Lord God will speak in me." *Here pause a while, and commune with your God.*

BEHOLD, O LORD, I POSSESS THEE, Who possessest all things, and Who canst do all things. Thou art the heavenly Physician of my soul, Who healest all my infirmities: and I am the sick man, whom Thou camest down from heaven to heal. Oh, heal my soul, for I have sinned against Thee.

ANIMA CHRISTI

SOUL OF CHRIST,
    be my sanctification.
Body of Christ, be my salvation.
Blood of Christ, fill all my veins.
Water of Christ's side,
    wash out my stains.
Passion of Christ, my comfort be.
O good Jesus, listen to me.
In Thy wounds I fain would hide,
Ne'er to be parted from Thy side.
Guard me should the foe assail me.
Call me when my life shall fail me.
Bid me come to Thee above,
With Thy saints to sing Thy love
World without end. Amen.

ANIMA CHRISTI,
    sanctifica me.
Corpus Christi, salva me.
Sanguis Christi, inebria me.
Aqua lateris Christi,
    lava me.
Passio Christi, conforta me.
O bone Jesu, exaudi me.
Intra tua vulnera absconde me.
Ne permittas me separari a te.
Ab hoste maligno defende me.
In hora mortis meae voca me.
Et jube me venire ad te,
Ut cum Sanctis tuis laudem te
In saecula saeculorum. Amen.

—BLESSED JOHN HENRY NEWMAN'S TRANSLATION

PALM SUNDAY

THE BLESSING OF THE PALMS
Dressed in red vestments, the Celebrant blesses the palm branches.

ANTIPHON *Matthew 21: 9*

HOSANNA *filio David: benedictus qui venit in nomine Domini. Rex Israel: Hosanna in excelsis!*

HOSANNA to the Son of David! Blessed is He that cometh in the Name of the Lord. O King of Israel: Hosanna in the highest!

COLLECT

BENE ✠ DIC, *quaesumus, Domine, hos palmarum (seu olivarum aut aliarum arborum) ramos: et praesta, ut quod populus tuus in tui venerationem hodierno die corporaliter agit, hoc spiritualiter summa devotione perficiat, de hoste victoriam reportando et opus misericordiae summopere diligendo. Per Christum Dominum nostrum.*

BLESS ✠, we beseech Thee, O Lord, these branches of palm: and grant that what Thy people today bodily perform for Thy honor, they may perfect spiritually with the utmost devotion, by gaining the victory over the enemy, and ardently loving every work of mercy. Through Christ our Lord.

All respond Amen. *The palms are distributed as psalms are sung with a responsory following each verse.*

PSALM 23: 1-2, 7-10

℣. DOMINI EST TERRA *et quae replent eam, orbis terrarum et qui habitant in eo. Nam ipse super maria fundavit eum, et super flumina firmavit eum.*

℣. THE EARTH IS THE LORD'S and the fullness thereof: the world and all they that dwell therein. For He hath founded it upon the seas: and hath prepared it from upon the rivers.

℟. *Pueri Hebræorum, portantes ramos olivarum, obviaverunt Domino, clamantes, et dicentes: Hosanna in excelsis.*

℟. The Hebrew children bearing olive branches, went forth to meet the Lord, crying out, and saying: Hosanna in the highest.

℣. Lift up your gates, O ye princes, and be ye lifted up, O eternal gates: and the king of glory shall enter in. Who is this king of glory? The Lord Who is strong and mighty: the Lord mighty in battle.

℟. The Hebrew children…

℣. Lift up your gates, O ye princes, and be ye lifted up, O eternal gates: and the king of glory shall enter in. Who is this king of glory? The Lord of hosts, He is the King of glory.

℟. The Hebrew children…

℣. Glory be to the Father, and to the Son, and to the Holy Ghost. As it was in the beginning, is now, and ever shall be, world without end. Amen.

℟. The Hebrew children…

℣. *Attollite, portae, capita vestra, et attollite vos, fores antiquae, ut ingrediatur rex glorias! Quis est iste rex gloriae? Dominus fortis et potens, Dominus potens in proelio.*

℟. *Pueri Hebræorum...*

℣. *Attollite, portae, capita vestra, et attollite vos, fores antiquae, ut ingrediatur rex gloriae! Quis est iste rex gloriae? Dominus exercituum: ipse est rex gloriae.*

℟. *Pueri Hebræorum...*

℣. *Gloria Patri, et Filio, et Spiritui Sancto, sicut erat in principio, et nunc, et semper, et in saecula saeculorum. Amen.*

℟. *Pueri Hebræorum...*

PSALM 46

℣. O CLAP YOUR HANDS, all ye people: shout unto God with the voice of joy. For the Lord is high, terrible: a great king over all the earth.

℟. The Hebrew children spread their garments in the way, and cried out, saying: Hosanna to the Son of God: blessed is He that cometh in the Name of the Lord.

℣. He hath subdued the people under us: and the nations under our feet. He

℣. OMNES POPULI, *plaudite manibus, exsultate Deo voce laetitiae, quoniam Dominus excelsus, terribilis, rex magnus super omnem terram.*

℟. *Pueri Hebraeorum vestimenta prosternebant in via, et clamabant dicentes: Hosanna filio David; benedictus qui venit in nomine Domini.*

℣. *Subicit populos nobis et nationes pedibus nostris. Eligit nobis hereditatem nostram gloriam Jacob, quem diligit.*

℟. *Pueri Hebraeorum vestimenta...*

℣. *Ascendit Deus cum exsultatione, Dominus cum voce tubae. Psallite Deo, psallite; psallite regi nostro, psallite.*

℟. *Pueri Hebraeorum vestimenta...*

℣. *Quoniam rex omnis terrae est Deus, psallite hymnum. Deus regnat super nationes, Deus sedet super solium sanctum suum.*

℟. *Pueri Hebraeorum vestimenta...*

℣. *Principes populorum congregati sunt cum populo Dei Abraham. Nam Dei sunt proceres terrae: excelsus est valde.*

℟. *Pueri Hebraeorum vestimenta...*

℣. *Gloria Patri, et Filio, et Spiritui Sancto, sicut erat in principio, et nunc, et semper, et in saecula saeculorum. Amen.*

℟. *Pueri Hebraeorum vestimenta...*

hath chosen for us our inheritance: the beauty of Jacob which He hath loved.

℟. The Hebrew children...

℣. God is ascended with jubilee: and the Lord with the sound of trumpet. Sing praises to God, sing ye: sing praises to our King, sing ye.

℟. The Hebrew children...

℣. For God is the King of all the earth: sing ye a hymn. God reigns over the nations: God sitteth on His holy throne.

℟. The Hebrew children...

℣. The princes of the people are gathered together: with the people of the God of Abraham. For the guardians of the earth are God's; He is exceedingly exalted.

℟. The Hebrew children...

℣. Glory be to the Father, and to the Son, and to the Holy Ghost. As it was in the beginning, is now, and ever shall be, world without end. Amen.

℟. The Hebrew children...

GOSPEL *Matthew 21: 1-9*

IN ILLO TEMPORE: Cum appropinquasset Jesus Jerosolymis, et venisset Bethphage ad montem Oliveti: tunc misit duos discipulos suos, dicens eis: Ite in castellum, quod contra

AT THAT TIME, when Jesus drew nigh to Jerusalem, and was come to Bethphage, unto Mount Olivet, then He sent two disciples, saying to them: Go ye into the village that is over against you, and immediately you shall find an ass tied, and a colt with her; loose them and bring them to Me; and if any man shall say anything to you, say ye that the Lord hath need of them; and forthwith he will let them go. Now all this was done that it might be fulfilled which was spoken by the prophet, saying: Tell ye the daughter of Sion: Behold thy King cometh to thee meek, and sitting upon an ass, and a colt the foal of her that is used to the yoke. And the disciples going did as Jesus commanded them. And they brought the ass and the colt, and laid their garments upon them, and made Him sit thereon. And a very great multitude spread their garments in the way, and others cut boughs from the trees and strewed them in the way, and the multitudes that went before and that followed cried, saying: Hosanna to the Son of David; Blessed is He that cometh in the Name of the Lord.

vos est, et statim invenietis asinam alligatam, et pullum cum ea: solvite, et adducite mihi: et si quis vobis aliquid dixerit, dicite quia Dominus his opus habet, et confestim dimittet eos. Hoc autem totum factum est, ut adimpleretur quod dictum est per prophetam, dicentem: Dicite filiae Sion: Ecce Rex tuus venit tibi mansuetus, sedens super asinam et pullum, filium subiugalis. Euntes autem discipuli, fecerunt sicut praecepit illis Jesus. Et adduxerunt asinam et pullum: et imposuerunt super eos vestimenta sua, et eum desuper sedere fecerunt. Plurima autem turba straverunt vestimenta sua in via: alii autem caedebant ramos de arboribus, et sternebant in via: turbae autem, quae praecedebant, et quae sequebantur, clamabant, dicentes: Hosanna filio David; benedictus qui venit in nomine Domini.

THE PROCESSION WITH BLESSED PALMS

℣. Let us go forth in peace.
℟. In the Name of Christ. Amen.

℣. *Procedamus in pace.*
℟. *In nomine Christi. Amen.*

1ST ANTIPHON

THE MULTITUDE WENT FORTH to meet the Redeemer with flowers and palms, and payeth the homage due to a triumphant Conqueror: the Gentiles proclaim the Son of God; and their voices

OCCURRUNT TURBAE cum floribus et palmis Redemptori obviam: et victori triumphanti digna dant obsequia: Filium Dei ore gentes praedicant: et in laudem Christi voces tonant

per nubila: Hosanna!

thunder through the skies in praise of Christ: Hosanna in the highest!

2ND ANTIPHON

CUM ANGELIS et pueris fideles invenia-mur, triumphatori mortis clamantes: Hosanna in excelsis!

LET THE FAITHFUL join with the Angels and children singing to the Conqueror of death: Hosanna in the highest!

3RD ANTIPHON

TURBA MULTA, quae convenerat ad diem festum, clamabat Domino: Benedictus qui venit in nomine Domini: Hosanna in excelsis!

A GREAT MULTITUDE that was met together at the festival cried out to the Lord: Blessed is He that cometh in the Name of the Lord: Hosanna in the highest!

4TH ANTIPHON

COEPERUNT omnes turbae descenden-tium gaudentes laudare Deum voce magna, super omnibus quas viderant virtutibus, dicentes: Benedictus qui venit Rex in nomine Domini; pax in terra, et gloria in excelsis!

NEAR THE DESCENT the whole multi-tude began with joy to praise God with a loud voice for all the mighty works they had seen, saying: Blessed be the King who cometh in the Name of the Lord; peace on earth and glory on high!

The hymn Gloria, Laus, et Honor is customarily sung at this time.

5TH ANTIPHON

OMNES COLLAUDANT nomen tuum, et dicunt: Benedictus qui venit in nomine Domini: Hosanna in excelsis!

ALL PRAISE Thy Name highly and say: Blessed is He who cometh in the Name of the Lord: Hosanna in the highest!

PSALM 147

LAUDA, Jerusalem, Dominum, lauda Deum tuum, Sion, quod firmavit seras portarum tuarum, benedixit filiis tuis in te. Composuit fines tuos in pace, medulla tritici satiat te. Emittit eloquium suum in terram, velociter currit verbum eius. Dat nivem sicut lanam, pruinam sicut cinerem spargit.

PRAISE the Lord, O Jerusalem: praise thy God, O Sion. Because He hath strengthened the bolts of thy gates: He hath blessed thy children within thee. Who hath placed peace in thy borders: and filleth thee with the fat of corn. Who sendeth forth His speech to the earth: His word runneth swiftly.

Who giveth snow like wool: scattereth mists like ashes. He sendeth His crystal like morsels: Who shall stand before the face of His cold? He shall send out His Word and shall melt them: His wind shall blow and the waters shall run. Who declareth His word to Jacob: His justice and His judgments to Israel. He hath not done in like manner to every nation: and His judgments He hath not made manifest to them.

Proicit glaciem suam ut frustula panis; coram frigore eius aquae rigescunt. Emittit verbum suum et liquefacit eas; flare iubet ventum suum et fluunt aquae. Annuntiavit verbum suum Jacob, statuta et praecepta sua Israel. Non fecit ita ulli nationi: praecepta sua non manifestavit eis.

The 5th Antiphon is repeated.

6TH ANTIPHON

WE ARE STREWN with the shining palms before the Lord as He approacheth; let us all run to meet Him with hymns and songs, glorify Him and say: Blessed be the Lord!

FULGENTIBUS PALMIS prosternimur advenienti Domino: huic omnes occurramus cum hymnis et canticis, glorificantes et dicentes: Benedictus Dominus!

7TH ANTIPHON

HAIL, OUR KING, O Son of David, O world's Redeemer, Whom prophets did foretell as the Savior to come of the house of Israel. For the Father sent Thee into the world as victim for salvation; from the beginning of the world all the saints awaited Thee: Hosanna now to the Son of David! Blessed be He who cometh in the Name of the Lord. Hosanna in the highest!

AVE, REX NOSTER, Fili David, Redemptor mundi, quem prophetae praedixerunt Salvatorem domui Israel esse venturum. Te enim ad salutarem victimam Pater misit in mundum, quem exspectabant omnes sancti ab origine mundi, et nunc: Hosanna Filio David. Benedictus qui venit in nomine Domini. Hosanna in excelsis!

8TH ANTIPHON

AS OUR LORD ENTERED the holy city, the Hebrew children, declaring the resurrection of life, with palm branches, cried

INGREDIENTE DOMINO in sanctam civitatem, Hebraeorum pueri resurrectionem vitae pronuntiantes, cum ramis

palmarum: Hosanna, clamabant, in
excelsis! Cum audisset populus, quod
Jesus veniret Jerosolymam, exierunt
obviam ei cum ramis palmarum:
Hosanna, clamabant, in excelsis!

out: Hosanna in the highest. When the
people heard that Jesus was coming
to Jerusalem, they went forth to meet
Him: with palm branches, cried out:
Hosanna in the highest!

COLLECT

DOMINE JESU CHRISTE, Rex ac
Redemptor noster, in cuius honorem,
hos ramos gestantes, solemnes laudes
decantavimus: concede propitius, ut
quocumque hi rami deportati fuerint,
ibi tuae benedictionis gratia descendat, et, quavis daemonum iniquitate
vel illusione profligata, dextera tua
protegat, quos redemit: Qui vivis
et regnas.

O LORD JESUS CHRIST, our King and
Redeemer, in whose honor we have
borne these palms and gone on prais-
ing Thee with song and solemnity: mercifully grant that whithersoever these
palms are taken, there the grace of
Thy blessing may descend; may every
wickedness and trick of the demons
be frustrated; and may Thy right hand
protect those it hath redeemed. Who
lives and reigns.

All respond Amen. The Celebrant and sacred ministers put on violet vestments for Mass.
The prayers at the foot of the altar are omitted.

≈ *Mass* ≈

INTROIT Psalm 21: 20, 22, 2

DOMINE, ne longe facias auxilium
tuum a me, ad defensionem meam
aspice: libera me de ore leonis, et a
cornibus unicornium humilitatem
meam. Deus, Deus meus, respice in
me: quare me dereliquisti? Longe a
salute mea verba delictorum meorum.
Domine, ne longe facias auxilium.

O LORD, keep not Thy help far from
me; look to my defense: deliver me
from the lion's mouth, and my lowness
from the horns of the unicorns. O God,
my God, look upon me; why hast Thou
forsaken me? Far from my salvation
are the words of my sins. O Lord, keep
not Thy help.

COLLECT

OMNIPOTENS sempiterne Deus,
qui humano generi, ad imitandum
humilitatis exemplum, Salvatorem

O ALMIGHTY and everlasting God, Who
didst cause our Savior to take upon Him
our flesh, and to undergo the Cross, for

an example of humility to be imitated by mankind; mercifully grant that we may deserve to possess not only the lessons of His patience, but also the fellowship of His Resurrection. Through the same Lord.

nostrum carnem sumere et crucem subire fecisti: concede propitius, ut et patientiae ipsius habere documenta et resurrectionis consortia mereamur. Per eundem Dominum.

EPISTLE *Philippians 2: 5-11*

BRETHREN, let this mind be in you which was also in Jesus Christ: Who being in the form of God, thought it not robbery to be equal with God; but emptied Himself, taking the form of a servant, being made in the likeness of men, and in habit found as a man. He humbled Himself, becoming obedient unto death, even to the death of the cross. For which cause God also hath exalted Him, and hath given Him a Name which is above all names: KNEEL that in the Name of Jesus every knee should bow, of those that are in Heaven, on earth, and under the earth: and that every tongue should confess that the Lord Jesus Christ is in the glory of God the Father.

FRATRES: Hoc enim sentite in vobis, quod et in Christo Jesu: qui, cum in forma Dei esset, non rapinam arbitratus est esse se aequalem Deo: sed semetipsum exinanivit, formam servi accipiens, in similitudinem hominum factus, et habitu inventus ut homo. Humiliavit semetipsum, factus oboediens usque ad mortem, mortem autem crucis. Propter quod et Deus exaltavit illum: et donavit illi nomen, quod est super omne nomen: ut in nomine Jesu omne genu flectatur caelestium, terrestrium et infernorum: et omnis lingua confiteatur, quia Dominus Jesus Christus in gloria est Dei Patris.

GRADUAL *Psalm 72: 24, 1-3*

THOU HAST HELD me by my right hand; and by Thy will Thou hast conducted me, and with Thy glory Thou hast received me. How good is God to Israel, to those of an upright heart! But my feet were almost moved, my steps had well-nigh slipped: because I was jealous of sinners, seeing the prosperity of sinners.

TENUISTI manum dexteram meam: et in voluntate tua deduxisti me: et cum gloria assumpsisti me. Quam bonus Israel Deus rectis corde! Mei autem paene moti sunt pedes: paene effusi sunt gressus mei: quia zelavi in peccatoribus, pacem peccatorum videns.

TRACT *Psalm 21: 2-9, 18, 19, 22, 24, 32*

DEUS, DEUS MEUS, réspice in me: quare me dereliquísti? Longe a salúte mea verba delictórum meórum. Deus meus, clamábo per diem, nec exáudies: in nocte, et non ad insipiéntiam mihi. Tu autem in sancto hábitas, laus Israël. In te speravérunt patres nostri: speravérunt, et liberásti eos. Ad te clamavérunt, et salvi facti sunt: in te speravérunt, et non sunt confúsi. Ego autem sum vermis, et non homo: oppróbrium hóminum et abjéctio plebis. Omnes qui vidébant me, aspernabántur me: locúti sunt lábiis et movérunt caput. Sperávit in Dómino, erípiat eum: salvum fáciat eum, quóniam vult eum. Ipsi vero consideravérunt et conspexérunt me: divisérunt sibi vestiménta mea, et super vestem meam misérunt sortem. Líbera me de ore leónis: et a córnibus unicórnium humilitátem meam. Qui timétis Dóminum, laudáte eum: univérsum semen Jacob, magnificáte eum. Annuntiábitur Dómino generátio ventúra: et annuntiábunt cæli justítiam ejus. Pópulo, qui nascétur, quem fecit Dóminus.

O GOD, MY GOD, look upon me; why hast Thou forsaken me? Far from my salvation are the words of my sins. O my God, I shall cry by day, and Thou wilt not hear; and by night, and it shall not be reputed as folly in me. But Thou dwellest in the holy place, the praise of Israel. In Thee have our fathers hoped: they have hoped, and Thou hast delivered them. They cried to Thee, and they were saved: they trusted in Thee, and were not confounded. But I am a worm, and no man: the reproach of men and the outcast of the people. All they that saw me have laughed me to scorn: they have spoken with the lips and wagged the head. He hoped in the Lord, let Him deliver him: let Him save him, seeing He delighteth in him. But they have looked and stared upon me: they parted my garments amongst them, and upon my vesture they cast lots. Deliver me from the lion's mouth: and my lowness from the horns of the unicorns. Ye that fear the Lord, praise Him: all ye the seed of Jacob, glorify Him. There shall be declared to the Lord a generation to come: and the heavens shall show forth His justice. To a people that shall be born, which the Lord hath made.

ILLUSTRATION BY DANIEL MITSUI

THE PASSION OF OUR LORD JESUS CHRIST
ACCORDING TO ST. MATTHEW

AT THAT TIME Jesus came with them into a country place which is called Gethsemani; and He said to His disciples: ✠ Sit you here, till I go yonder and pray. And taking with Him Peter and the two sons of Zebedee, He began to grow sorrowful and to be sad. Then He saith to them: ✠ My soul is sorrowful even unto death; stay you here and watch with Me. And going a little further, He fell upon His face, praying and saying: ✠ My Father, if it be possible, let this chalice pass from Me. Nevertheless, not as I will, but as Thou wilt. And He cometh to His disciples, and findeth them asleep. And He saith to Peter: ✠ What! Could you not watch one hour with Me? Watch ye, and pray that ye enter not into temptation. The

IN ILLO TÉMPORE: Venit Jesus cum illis in villam, quæ dícitur Gethsémani, et dixit discípulis suis: ✠ *Sedéte hic, donec vadam illuc, et orem. Et assúmpto Petro, et duóbus fíliis Zebedaéi, cœpit contristári et mœstus esse. Tunc ait illis:* ✠ *Tristis est ánima mea usque ad mortem: sustinéte hic, et vigiláte mecum. Et progréssus pusíllum, prócidit in fáciem suam, orans, et dicens:* ✠ *Pater mi, si possíbile est, tránseat a me calix iste. Verúmtamen non sicut ego volo, sed sicut tu. Et venit ad discípulos suos, et invénit eos dormiéntes: et dicit Petro:* ✠ *Sic non potuístis una hora vigiláre mecum? Vigiláte, et oráte ut non intrétis in tentatiónem. Spíritus quidem promptus est, caro autem infírma. Íterum secúndo ábiit, et orávit, dicens: ✠ Pater mi, si non potest hic calix transíre, nisi bibam illum, fiat volúntas tua. Et venit íterum, et invénit eos dormiéntes: erant enim óculi eórum graváti. Et relíctis illis, íterum ábiit, et orávit tértio, eúmdem sermónem dicens. Tunc venit ad discípulos suos, et dicít ills: ✠ Dormíte jam, et requiéscite: ecce appropinquávit hora, et Fílius hóminis tradétur in manus peccatórum. Súrgite, eámus: ecce appropinquávit qui me tradet. Adhuc eo loquénte, ecce Judas unus de duódecim venit, et cum eo turba multa cum gládiis et fústibus, missi a princípibus sacerdótum, et senióribus pópuli. Qui autem trádidit eum, dedit illis signum dicens: Quemcúmque osculátus fúero, ipse est, tenéte eum. Et conféstim accédens ad Jesum, dixit: Ave, Rabbi. Et osculátus est eum. Dixítque illi Jesus: ✠ Amíce, ad quid venísti? Tunc accessérunt, et manus injecérunt in Jesum, et tenuérunt eum. Et ecce unus ex his, qui erant cum Jesu, exténdens manum, exémit gládium suum, et percútiens servum príncipis sacerdótum, amputávit aurículam ejus. Tunc ait illi Jesus: ✠ Convérte gládium tuum in locum suum. Omnes enim, qui accéperint gládium, gládio períbunt. An putas quia non possum rogáre Patrem meum, et exhibébit mihi modo plus quam duódecim*

spirit indeed is willing, but the flesh is weak. Again the second time, He went and prayed, saying: ✠ My Father, if this chalice may not pass away, but I must drink it, Thy will be done. And He cometh again, and findeth them sleeping: for their eyes were heavy. And leaving them, He went again and He prayed the third time, saying the selfsame word. Then He cometh to His disciples, and saith to them: ✠ Sleep ye now and take your rest: behold, the hour is at hand, and the Son of Man shall be betrayed into the hands of sinners. Rise, let us go: behold, he is at hand that will betray Me. As He yet spoke, behold Judas, one of the twelve, came, and with him a great multitude with swords and clubs, sent from the chief priests and the ancients of the people. And he that betrayed Him gave them a sign, saying: Whomsoever I shall kiss, that is He: hold Him fast. And forthwith coming to Jesus, he said: Hail, Rabbi. And he kissed Him. And Jesus said to Him: ✠ Friend, whereto art thou come? Then they came up and laid hands on Jesus, and held Him. And behold one of them that were with Jesus, stretching forth his hand, drew out his sword, and striking the servant of the high priest, cut off his ear. Then Jesus saith to him: ✠ Put up again thy sword into its place; for all that take the sword shall perish with the sword. Thinkest thou that I cannot ask My Father, and He will give Me presently more than twelve legions of Angels? How then shall the Scriptures be fulfilled, that so it must be done? In that same hour Jesus said to the multitudes: ✠ You are come out as it were to a robber with swords and clubs to apprehend Me. I sat daily with you, teaching in the temple, and you laid not hands on Me. Now all this was done that the Scriptures of the prophets might be fulfilled. Then the disciples, all leaving Him, fled. But they holding Jesus led Him to Caiphas the high priest, where the scribes and the ancients were assembled. And Peter followed Him afar off, even to the court of the high priest. And going in, he sat with the servants, that he might see the end. And the chief priests and the whole council sought false witness against Jesus, that they might put Him to death. And they found none, whereas many false witnesses had come in. And last of all there came two false witnesses; and they said: This man said, I am able to destroy the temple of God, and after three days to rebuild it. And the high priest, rising up, said to Him: Answerest Thou nothing to the things which these witness against Thee? But Jesus held His peace. And the high priest said to Him: I adjure Thee by the living God, that Thou tell us if Thou be the Christ the Son of God. Jesus saith to him: ✠

legiónes Angelórum? Quómodo ergo implebúntur Scriptúræ, quia sic opórtet fíeri? In illa hora dixit Jesus turbis: ✠ Tamquam ad latrónem exístis cum gládiis et fústibus comprehéndere me: quotídie apud vos sedébam docens in templo, et non me tenuístis. Hoc autem totum factum est, ut adimpleréntur Scriptúræ prophetárum. Tunc discípuli omnes, relícto eo, fugérunt. At illi tenéntes Jesum, duxérunt ad Cáipham príncipem sacerdótum, ubi scribæ et senióres convénerant. Petrus autem sequebátur eum a longe, usque in átrium príncipis sacerdótum. Et ingréssus intro, sedébat cum minístris, ut vidéret finem. Príncipes autem sacerdótum, et omne concílium, quærébant falsum testimónium contra Jesum, ut eum morti tráderent: et non invenérunt, cum multi falsi testes accessíssent. Novíssime autem venérunt duo falsi testes, et dixérunt: Hic dixit: Possum destrúere templum Dei, et post tríduum reædificáre illud. Et surgens princeps sacerdótum, ait illi: Nihil respóndes ad ea, quæ isti advérsum te testificántur? Jesus autem tacébat. Et princeps sacerdótum ait illi: Adjúro te per Deum vivum, ut dicas nobis, si tu es Christus Fílius Dei. Dicit illi Jesus: ✠ Tu dixísti. Verúmtamen dico vobis, ámodo vidébitis Fílium hóminis sedéntem a dextris virtútis Dei, et veniéntem in núbibus cæli. Tunc princeps sacerdótum scidit vestiménta sua, dicens: Blasphemávit: quid adhuc egémus téstibus? Ecce nunc audístis blasphémiam: quid vobis vidétur? At illi respondéntes dixérunt: Reus est mortis. Tunc exspuérunt in fáciem ejus, et cólaphis eum cecidérunt, álii autem palmas in fáciem ejus dedérunt, dicéntes: Prophetíza nobis, Christe, quis est qui te percússit? Petrus vero sedébat foris in átrio: et accéssit ad eum una ancílla, dicens: Et tu cum Jesu Galilaéo eras. At ille negávit coram ómnibus, dicens: Néscio quid dicis. Exeúnte autem illo jánuam, vidit eum ália ancílla, et aít his qui erant ibi: Et hic erat cum Jesu Nazaréno. Et íterum negávit cum juraménto: Quia non novi hóminem. Et post pusíllum accessérunt qui stabant, et dixérunt Petro: Vere et tu ex illis es: nam et loquéla tua maniféstum te facit. Tunc cœpit detestári, et juráre quia non novísset hóminem. Et contínuo gallus cantávit. Et recordátus est Petrus verbi Jesu, quod díxerat: ✠ Priúsquam gallus cantet, ter me negábis. Et egréssus foras, flevit amáre. Mane autem facto, consílium iniérunt omnes príncipes sacerdótum, et senióres pópuli advérsus Jesum, ut eum morti tráderent. Et vinctum adduxérunt eum, et tradidérunt Póntio Piláto praésidi. Tunc videns Judas, qui eum

Thou hast said it. Nevertheless I say to you, hereafter you shall see the Son of Man sitting on the right hand of the power of God, and coming in the clouds of heaven. Then the high priest rent his garments, saying: He hath blasphemed; what further need have we of witnesses? Behold, now you have heard the blasphemy. What think you? But they answering, said: He is guilty of death. Then they did spit in His face and buffeted Him; and others struck His face with the palms of their hands, saying: Prophesy unto us, O Christ, who is he that struck Thee? But Peter sat without in the court, and there came to him a maid-servant, saying: Thou also wast with Jesus the Galilean. But he denied before them all, saying: I know not what thou sayest. And as he went out of the gate, another maid saw him, and she saith to them that were there: This man also was with Jesus of Nazareth. And again he denied with an oath: I know not the man. And after a little while, they came that stood by and said to Peter: Surely thou also art one of them; for even thy speech doth discover thee. Then he began to curse and to swear that he knew not the man; and immediately the cock crew. And Peter remembered the word of Jesus which He had said: ✠ Before the cock crow, thou wilt deny Me thrice. And going forth, he wept bitterly. And when morning was come, all the chief priests and ancients of the people took counsel against Jesus, that they might put Him to death. And they brought Him bound, and delivered Him to Pontius Pilate the governor. Then Judas, who betrayed Him, seeing that He was condemned, repenting himself, brought back the thirty pieces of silver to the chief priests and ancients, saying: I have sinned in betraying innocent blood. But they said: What is that to us? Look thou to it. And casting down the pieces of silver in the temple, he departed, and went and hanged himself with a halter. But the chief priests having taken the pieces of silver, said: It is not lawful to put them into the corbona, because it is the price of blood. And after they had consulted together, they bought with them the potter's field, to be a burying place for strangers. For this cause that field was called Haceldama, that is, the field of blood, even to this day. Then was fulfilled that which was spoken by Jeremiah the prophet, saying: And they took the thirty pieces of silver, the price of Him that was prized, whom they prized of the children of Israel: and they gave them unto the potter's field, as the Lord appointed to me. And Jesus stood before the governor, and the governor asked Him, saying: Art Thou the King of the Jews? Jesus saith to him: ✠ Thou sayest it. And when He was accused by the

trádidit, quod damnátus esset, pœniténtia ductus, rétulit trigínta argénteos princípibus sacerdótum et senióribus, dicens: Peccávi, tradens sánguinem justum. At illi dixérunt: Quid ad nos? Tu víderis. Et projéctis argénteis in templo, recéssit: et ábiens, láqueo se suspéndit. Príncipes autem sacerdótum, accéptis argénteis, dixérunt: Non licet eos míttere in córbonam: quia prétium sánguinis est. Consílio autem ínito, emérunt ex illis agrum fíguli, in sepultúram peregrinórum. Propter hoc vocátus est ager ille Hacéldama, hoc est, ager sánguinis, usque in hodiérnum diem. Tunc implétum est, quod dictum est per Jeremíam prophétam, dicéntem: Et accepérunt trigínta argénteos prétium appretiáti, quem appretiavérunt a fíliis Israël: et dedérunt eos in agrum fíguli, sicut constítuit mihi Dóminus. Jesus autem stetit ante praésidem, et interrogávit eum præses, dicens: Tu es Rex Judæórum? Dicit illi Jesus: ✠ Tu dicis. Et cum accusarétur a princípibus sacerdótum et senióribus, nihil respóndit. Tunc dicit illi Pilátus: Non audis quanta advérsum te dicunt testimónia? Et non respóndit ei ad ullum verbum, ita ut mirarétur præses veheménter. Per diem autem solémnem consuéverat præses pópulo dimíttere unum vinctum, quem voluíssent. Habébat autem tunc vinctum insígnem, qui

dicebátur Barábbas. Congregátis ergo
illis, dixit Pilátus: Quem vultis dimít-
tam vobis: Barábbam, an Jesum, qui
dícitur Christus? Sciébat enim quod
per invídiam tradidíssent eum. Sedénte
autem illo pro tribunáli, misit ad eum
uxor ejus, dicens: Nihil tibi et justo
illi: multa enim passa sum hódie per
visum propter eum. Príncipes autem
sacerdótum et senióres persuasérunt
pópulis ut péterent Barábbam, Jesum
vero pérderent. Respóndens autem
præses ait illis: Quem vultis vobis de
duóbus dimítti? At illi dixérunt:
Barábbam. Dicit illis Pilátus: Quid
ígitur fáciam de Jesu, qui dícitur
Christus? Dicunt omnes: Crucifigátur.
Ait illis præses: Quid enim mali fecit?
At illi magis clamábant, dicéntes:
Crucifigátur. Videns autem Pilátus
quia nihil profíceret, sed magis tumúl-
tus fíeret: accépta aqua, lavit manus
coram pópulo, dicens: Ínnocens ego
sum a sánguine justi hujus: vos vidéri-
tis. Et respóndens univérsus pópulus,
dixit: Sanguis ejus super nos, et super
fílios nostros. Tunc dimísit illis
Barábbam: Jesum autem flagellátum
trádidit eis, ut crucifigerétur. Tunc
mílites praésidis suscipiéntes Jesum
in prætórium, congregavérunt ad eum
univérsam cohórtem: et exuéntes eum,
chlámydem coccíneam circumdedérunt
ei: et plecténtes corónam de spinis,
posuérunt super caput ejus, et

chief priests and ancients, He answered
nothing. Then Pilate saith to Him: Dost
not Thou hear how great testimonies
they allege against Thee? And He
answered to him never a word, so that
the governor wondered exceedingly.
Now upon the solemn day the governor
was accustomed to release to the people
one prisoner, whom they wished. And
he had then a notorious prisoner that
was called Barabbas. They therefore
being gathered together, Pilate said:
Whom will you that I release to you:
Barabbas, or Jesus that is called Christ?
For he knew that for envy they had
delivered Him. And as he was sitting
in the place of judgment, his wife sent
to him, saying: Have thou nothing to
do with that just man, for I have suffered
many things this day in a dream because
of Him. But the chief priests and
ancients persuaded the people that they
should ask Barabbas, and make Jesus
away. And the governor answering, said
to them: Whether will you of the two
to be released unto you? But they said:
Barabbas. Pilate saith to them: What
shall I do then with Jesus that is called
Christ? They say all: Let Him be crucified. The governor said to them: Why,
what evil hath He done? But they cried
out the more, saying: Let Him be crucified. And Pilate seeing that he prevailed
nothing, but that rather a tumult was
made, taking water, washed his hands

before the people, saying: I am innocent of the blood of this just man; look you to it. And the whole people, answering, said: His blood be upon us and upon our children. Then he released to them Barabbas: and having scourged Jesus, delivered Him unto them to be crucified.Then the soldiers of the governor, taking Jesus into the hall, gathered together unto Him the whole band; and stripping Him, they put a scarlet cloak about Him; and plaiting a crown of thorns, they put it upon His head and a reed in His right hand. And bowing the knee before Him, they mocked Him, saying: Hail, King of the Jews. And spitting upon Him, they took the reed and struck His head. And after they had mocked Him, they took off the cloak from Him, and put on Him His own garments, and led Him away to crucify Him. And going out, they found a man of Cyrene, named Simon: him they forced to take up His cross. And they came to the place that is called Golgotha, which is the place of Calvary. And they gave Him wine to drink mingled with gall: and when He had tasted, He would not drink. And after they had crucified Him, they divided His garments, casting lots; that it might be fulfilled which was spoken by the prophet, saying: They divided My garments among them, and upon My vesture they cast lots. And they sat and

arúndinem in déxtera ejus. Et genu flexo ante eum, illudébant ei, dicéntes: Ave, Rex Judæórum. Et exspuéntes in eum, accepérunt arúndinem, et percutiébant caput ejus. Et postquam illusérunt ei, exuérunt eum chlámyde, et induérunt eum vestiméntis ejus, et duxérunt eum ut crucifígerent. Exeúntes autem, invenérunt hóminem Cyrenaéum, nómine Simónem: hunc angariavérunt, ut tólleret crucem ejus. Et venérunt in locum qui dícitur Gólgotha, quod est Calváriæ locus. Et dedérunt ei vinum bíbere cum felle mixtum. Et cum gustásset, nóluit bíbere. Postquam autem crucifixérunt eum, divisérunt vestiménta ejus, sortem mitténtes: ut implerétur quod dictum est per prophétam, dicéntem: Divisérunt sibi vestiménta mea, et super vestem meam misérunt sortem. Et sedéntes, servábant eum. Et imposuérunt super caput ejus causam ipsíus scriptam: Hic est Jesus Rex Judæórum. Tunc crucifíxi sunt cum eo duo latrónes: unus a dextris, et unus a sinístris. Prætereúntes autem blasphemábant eum, movéntes cápita sua, et dicéntes: Vah, qui déstruis templum Dei, et in tríduo illud reædíficas: salva temetípsum. Si Fílius Dei es, descende de cruce. Simíliter et príncipes sacerdótum illudéntes cum scribis et senióribus, dicébant: Alios salvos fecit, seípsum non potest salvum fácere: si Rex Israël est, descéndat nunc de cruce, et crédimus ei: confídit in Deo: líberet nunc, si vult eum; dixit enim: Quia Fílius Dei sum. Idípsum autem et latrónes, qui crucifíxi erant cum eo, improperábant ei. A sexta autem hora ténebræ factæ sunt super univérsam terram, usque ad horam nonam. Et circa horam nonam clamávit Jesus voce magna, dicens: ✠ *Eli, Eli, lamma sabactháni? Hoc est:* ✠ *Deus meus, Deus meus, ut quid dereliquísti me? Quidam autem illic stantes, et audiéntes, dicébant: Elíam vocat iste. Et contínuo currens unus ex eis, accéptam spóngiam implévit acéto, et impósuit arúndini, et dabat ei bíbere. Céteri vero dicébant: Sine, videámus an véniat Elías líberans eum. Jesus autem íterum clamans voce magna, emísit spíritum. Et ecce velum templi scissum est in duas partes a summo usque deórsum: et terra mota est, et petræ scissæ sunt, et monuménta apérta sunt: et multa córpora sanctórum, qui dormíerant, surrexérunt. Et exeúntes de monuméntis post resurrectiónem ejus, venérunt in sanctam civitátem, et apparuérunt multis. Centúrio autem et qui cum eo erant custodiéntes Jesum, viso terræmótu et his quæ fiébant, timuérunt valde, dicéntes: Vere Fílius Dei erat iste. Erant autem ibi mulíeres multæ a longe, quæ secútæ erant Jesum a*

watched Him. And they put over His head His cause written: This is Jesus, the King of the Jews. There were crucified with Him two thieves: one on the right hand and one on the left. And they that passed by blasphemed Him, wagging their heads, and saying: Vah, Thou that destroyest the temple of God and in three days dost rebuild it, save Thine own self. If Thou be the Son of God, come down from the cross. In like manner also the chief priests with the scribes and ancients, mocking, said: He saved others, Himself He cannot save: if He be the King of Israel, let Him now come down from the cross, and we will believe Him; He trusted in God, let Him now deliver Him if He will have Him; for He said: I am the Son of God. And the self-same thing the thieves also that were crucified with Him reproached Him with. Now from the sixth hour there was darkness over the whole earth, until the ninth hour. And about the ninth hour, Jesus cried with a loud voice, saying: ✠ Eli, Eli, lamma sabacthani? That is: ✠ My God, My God, why hast Thou forsaken Me? And some that stood there and heard, said: This man calleth Elias. And immediately one of them running took a sponge and filled it with vinegar and put it on a reed and gave Him to drink. And the others said: Let be; let us see whether Elias will come to deliver Him. And Jesus again crying with a loud voice, yielded up the ghost. KNEEL AND PAUSE And behold the veil of the temple was rent in two from the top even to the bottom; and the earth quaked and the rocks were rent; and the graves were opened, and many bodies of the saints that had slept arose, and coming out of the tombs after His resurrection, came into the holy city, and appeared to many. Now the centurion and they that were with him watching Jesus, having seen the earthquake and the things that were done, were sore afraid, saying: Indeed this was the Son of God. And there were there many women afar off, who had

Galilaéa, ministrántes ei: inter quas erat María Magdaléne, et María Jacóbi et Joseph mater, et mater filiórum Zebedaéi. Cum autem sero factum esset, venit quidam homo dives ab Arimathaéa, nómine Joseph, qui et ipse discípulus erat Jesu. Hic accéssit ad Pilátum, et pétiit corpus Jesu. Tunc Pilátus jussit reddi corpus. Et accépto córpore, Joseph invólvit illud in síndone munda. Et pósuit illud in monuménto suo novo, quod excíderat in petra. Et advólvit saxum magnum ad óstium monuménti, et ábiit.

followed Jesus from Galilee, ministering unto Him: among whom was Mary Magdalen, and Mary the Mother of James and Joseph, and the mother of the sons of Zebedee. And when it was evening, there came a certain rich man of Arimathea, named Joseph, who also himself was a disciple of Jesus. He went to Pilate and asked the body of Jesus. Then Pilate commanded that the body should be delivered. And Joseph taking the body, wrapt it up in a clean linen cloth, and laid it in his own new monument, which he had hewed out in a rock. And he rolled a great stone to the door of the monument and went his way.

OFFERTORY *Psalm 68: 21, 22*

MY HEART HATH EXPECTED reproach and misery; and I looked for one that would grieve together with Me, but there was none: I sought for one that would comfort Me, and I found none: and they gave Me gall for My food, and in My thirst they gave Me vinegar to drink.

IMPROPÉRIUM exspectávit cor meum et misériam: et sustínui qui simul mecum contristarétur, et non fuit: consolántem me quæsívi, et non invéni: et dedérunt in escam meam fel, et in siti mea potavérunt me acéto.

SECRET

CONCÉDE, quaésumus, Dómine: ut óculis tuæ majestátis munus oblátum, et grátiam nobis devotiónis obtíneat, et efféctum beátæ perennitátis acquírat. Per Dóminum nostrum.

GRANT, we beseech Thee, O Lord, that the gifts offered in the sight of Thy majesty, may procure us the grace of devotion and obtain for us the fruit of a blessed eternity. Through our Lord.

PREFACE OF THE HOLY CROSS

VERE DIGNUM ET IUSTUM EST, aequum et salutare, nos tibi semper et ubique gratias agere: Domine, sancte Pater, omnipotens aeterne Deus: Qui salutem humani generis in ligno Crucis constituisti: ut unde mors oriebatur, inde vita resurgeret: et, qui in ligno vincebat, in ligno quoque vinceretur: per Christum Dominum nostrum. Per quem maiestatem tuam laudant Angeli, adorant Dominationes, tremunt Potestates. Caeli caelorumque Virtutes, ac beata Seraphim, socia exsultatione concelebrant. Cum quibus et nostras voces ut admitti iubeas, deprecamur, supplici confessione dicentes...

IT IS TRULY MEET AND JUST, right and for our salvation, that we should at all times, and in all places, give thanks unto Thee, O holy Lord, Father almighty, everlasting God: Who didst establish the salvation of mankind on the tree of the Cross: that whence death came, thence also life might arise again, and that he who overcame by the tree, by the tree also might be overcome, through Christ our Lord. Through Whom the Angels praise Thy Majesty, the Dominions worship it, the Powers stand in awe. The heavens and the heavenly hosts together with the blessed Seraphim in triumphant chorus unite to celebrate it. Together with these we entreat Thee, that Thou mayest bid our voices also to be admitted while we say with lowly praise...

COMMUNION *Matthew 26: 42*

PATER, si non potest hic calix transíre, nisi bibam illum, fíat volúntas tua.

FATHER, if this chalice may not pass away, lest I drink it, Thy Will be done.

POSTCOMMUNION

BY THE OPERATION of this Mystery, O Lord, may our vices be cleansed, and our just desires fulfilled. Through our Lord.

PER HUJUS, Dómine, operatiónem mystérii: et vítia nostra purgéntur, et justa desidéria compleántur. Per Dóminum nostrum.

MAUNDY THURSDAY

White and Violet   *First Class*

INTROIT *Galatians 6: 14; Psalm 66: 2*

BUT IT BEHOOVES US to glory in the Cross of our Lord Jesus Christ: in Whom is our salvation, life, and resurrection: by Whom we are saved and delivered. May God have mercy on us, and bless us: may He cause the light of His countenance to shine upon us; and may He have mercy on us. But it behooves us to glory.

NOS AUTEM gloriári opórtet in Cruce Dómini nostri Jesu Christi: in quo est salus, vita et resurréctio nostra: per quem salváti et liberáti sumus. Deus misereátur nostri, et benedícat nobis: illúminet vultum suum super nos, et misereátur nostri. Nos autem. Glória Patri. Nos autem gloriári opórtet.

COLLECT

O GOD, from Whom Judas received the punishment of his guilt, and the thief the reward of his confession, grant us the effect of Thy clemency; that even as in His passion our Lord Jesus Christ gave to each a different recompense according to his merits, so may He deliver us from our old sins and grant us the grace of His resurrection. Who with Thee lives and reigns.

DEUS, a quo et Judas reátus sui pœnam, et confessiónis suæ latro praémium sumpsit, concéde nobis tuæ propitiatiónis efféctum: ut, sicut in passióne sua Jesus Christus Dóminus noster divérsa utrísque íntulit stipéndia meritórum; ita nobis, abláto vetustátis erróre, resurrectiónis suæ grátiam largiátur: Qui tecum vivit et regnat.

EPISTLE *I Corinthians 11: 20-32*

BRETHREN: When you come therefore into one place, it is not now to eat

FRATRES: Convenientibus vobis in unum, iam non est dominicam

cenam manducare. Unusquisque enim suam cenam praesumit ad manducandum. Et alius quidem esurit, alius autem ebrius est. Numquid domos non habetis ad manducandum et bibendum? Aut ecclesiam Dei contemnitis, et confunditis eos, qui non habent? Quid dicam vobis? Laudo vos? In hoc non laudo. Ego enim accepi a Domino, quod et tradidi vobis, quoniam Dominus Jesus, in qua nocte tradebatur, accepit panem, et gratias agens fregit, et dixit: Accipite, et manducate: hoc est corpus meum, quod pro vobis tradetur: hoc facite in meam commemorationem. Similiter et calicem, postquam cenavit, dicens: Hic calix novum testamentum est in meo sanguine: hoc facite, quotiescumque bibetis, in meam commemorationem. Quotiescumque enim manducabitis panem hunc, et calicem bibetis: mortem Domini annuntiabitis, donec veniat. Itaque quicumque manducaverit panem hunc vel biberit calicem Domini indigne, reus erit corporis et sanguinis Domini. Probet autem seipsum homo: et sic de pane illo edat et de calice bibat. Qui enim manducat et bibit indigne, iudicium sibi manducat et bibit, non diiudicans corpus Domini. Ideo inter vos multi infirmi et imbecilles, et dormiunt multi. Quod si nosmetipsos diiudicaremus, non utique iudicaremur. Dum iudicamur

the Lord's supper. For every one taketh before his own supper to eat. And one indeed is hungry and another is drunk. What, have you not houses to eat and to drink in? Or despise ye the church of God and put them to shame that have not? What shall I say to you? Do I praise you? In this I praise you not. For I have received of the Lord that which I also delivered unto you, that the Lord Jesus, the same night in which He was betrayed, took bread, and giving thanks, broke and said: Take ye and eat: This is My Body, which shall be delivered for you. This do for the commemoration of Me. In like manner also the chalice, after He had supped, saying: This chalice is the new testament in My Blood. This do ye, as often as you shall drink, for the commemoration of Me. For as often as you shall eat this bread and drink the chalice, you shall show the death of the Lord, until He come. Therefore, whosoever shall eat this bread, or drink the chalice of the Lord unworthily, shall be guilty of the Body and the Blood of the Lord. But let a man prove himself; and so let him eat of that bread and drink of the chalice. For he that eateth and drinketh unworthily eateth and drinketh judgment to himself, not discerning the Body of the Lord. Therefore are there many infirm and weak among you: and many sleep. But if we would judge ourselves, we should not be judged. But whilst we are judged, we are chastised by the Lord, that we be not condemned with this world.

autem, a Domino corripimur, ut non cum hoc mundo damnemur.

GRADUAL Philippians 2: 8-9

CHRIST BECAME obedient for us unto death, even to the death of the cross. For which cause God also exalted Him and hath given Him a Name which is above all names.

CHRISTUS FACTUS EST pro nobis oboediens usque ad mortem, mortem autem crucis. Propter quod et Deus exaltavit illum: et dedit illi nomen, quod est super omne nomen.

GOSPEL John 13: 1-15

BEFORE THE FESTIVAL-DAY of the Pasch, Jesus knowing that His hour was come, that He should pass out of this world to the Father, having loved His own who were in the world, He loved them unto the end. And when supper was done (the devil having now put into the heart of Judas, the son of Simon the Iscariot, to betray Him), knowing that the Father had given Him all things into His hands and that He came from God and goeth to God: He riseth from supper and layeth aside His garments and, having taken a towel, girded Himself. After that, He putteth water into a basin and began to wash the feet of the disciples and to wipe them with the towel wherewith He was girded. He cometh therefore to Simon Peter. And Peter saith to Him: Lord, dost Thou wash my feet? Jesus answered and said to him: What I do, thou knowest not now: but thou shalt know hereafter. Peter saith to Him: Thou

ANTE DIEM FESTUM Paschae, sciens Jesus quia venit hora eius, ut transeat ex hoc mundo ad Patrem, cum dilexisset suos, qui erant in mundo, in finem dilexit eos. Et cena facta, cum diabolus iam misisset in cor, ut traderet eum Judas Simonis Iscariotae, sciens quia omnia dedit ei Pater in manus, et quia a Deo exivit, et ad Deum vadit, surgit a cena, et ponit vestimenta sua, et cum accepisset linteum, praecinxit se. Deinde mittit aquam in pelvim, et coepit lavare pedes discipulorum, et extergere linteo, quo erat praecinctus. Venit ergo ad Simonem Petrum. Et dicit ei Petrus: Domine, tu mihi lavas pedes? Respondit Jesus, et dixit ei: Quod ego facio, tu nescis modo, scies autem postea. Dicit ei Petrus: Non lavabis mihi pedes in aeternum. Respondit ei Jesus: Si non lavero te, non habebis partem mecum. Dicit ei Simon Petrus: Domine, non tantum pedes meos, sed et manus et caput.

Dicit ei Jesus: Qui lotus est, non indiget nisi ut pedes lavet, sed est mundus totus. Et vos mundi estis, sed non omnes. Sciebat enim quisnam esset qui traderet eum; propterea dixit: Non estis mundi omnes. Postquam ergo lavit pedes eorum, et accepit vestimenta sua, cum recubuisset iterum, dixit eis: Scitis quid fecerim vobis? Vos vocatis me Magister et Domine, et bene dicitis; sum etenim. Si ergo ego lavi pedes vestros, Dominus et Magister: et vos debetis alter alterius lavare pedes. Exemplum enim dedi vobis, ut, quemadmodum ego feci vobis, ita et vos faciatis.

shalt never wash my feet. Jesus answered him: If I wash thee not, thou shalt have no part with Me. Simon Peter saith to Him: Lord, not only my feet, but also my hands and my head. Jesus saith to him: He that is washed needeth not but to wash his feet, but is clean wholly. And you are clean, but not all. For He knew who he was that would betray Him; therefore He said: You are not all clean. Then after He had washed their feet and taken His garments, being set down again, He said to them: Know you what I have done to you? You call Me Master and Lord. And you say well; for so I am. If then I being your Lord and Master, have washed your feet, you also ought to wash one another's feet. For I have given you an example, that as I have done to you, so you do also.

THE MAUNDY OR WASHING OF THE FEET

During the ceremony the following antiphons are recited or sung.

1ST ANTIPHON *John 13: 34; Psalm 118: 1*

A NEW COMMANDMENT I give unto you: That you love one another, as I have loved you, saith the Lord. Blessed are the undefiled in the way: who walk in the law of the Lord.

MANDATUM NOVUM do vobis: ut diligatis invicem, sicut dilexi vos, dicit Dominus. Beati immaculati in via: qui ambulant in lege Domini.

2ND ANTIPHON *John 13: 4-5, 15; Psalm 47: 2*

AFTER our Lord was risen from supper, He put water into a basin, and began to wash the feet of His disciples: to whom He gave this example. Great is the Lord, and exceedingly to be praised in the city of our God, in His holy mountain. After the Lord was risen.

POSTQUAM surrexit Dominus a cena, misit aquam in pelvim, et coepit lavare pedes discipulorum: hoc exemplum reliquit eis. Magnus Dominus, et laudabilis nimis: in civitate Dei nostri, in monte sancto eius. Postquam surrexit Dominus.

3RD ANTIPHON *John 13: 12-13, 15: Psalm 84: 2*

OUR LORD JESUS, after He had supped with His disciples, washed their feet, and said to them: Know you what I your Lord and Master have done to you? I have given you an example, that ye also may do likewise. Thou hast blessed, O Lord, Thy land; Thou hast turned away the captivity of Jacob.

DOMINUS JESUS, postquam cenavit cum discipulis suis, lavit pedes eorum, et ait illis: Scitis quid fecerim vobis ego, Dominus et Magister? Exemplum dedi vobis, ut et vos ita faciatis. Benedixisti, Domine, terram tuam: avertisti captivitatem Iacob.

4TH ANTIPHON *John 13: 6-8*

LORD, dost Thou wash my feet? Jesus answered and said to them: If I shall not wash thy feet, thou shalt have no part with Me. He came to Simon Peter, and Peter said to Him: Lord, dost Thou wash my feet? Jesus answered and said to them: If I shall

DOMINE, tu mihi lavas pedes? Respondit Jesus, et dixit ei: Si non lavero tibi pedes, non habebis partem mecum. Venit ergo ad Simonem Petrum, et dixit ei Petrus. Domine, tu mihi lavas pedes? Respondit Jesus, et dixit ei: Si non lavero tibi pedes,

non habebis partem mecum. Quod
ego facio, tu nescis modo: scies autem
postea.

not wash thy feet, thou shalt have
no part with Me. What I do, thou
knowest not now; but thou shalt
know hereafter.

5TH ANTIPHON *John 13: 14; Psalm 48: 2*

SI EGO, *Dominus et Magister vester,*
lavi vobis pedes: quanto magis debetis
alter alterius lavare pedes? Audite haec,
omnes gentes: auribus percipite, qui
habitatis orbem.

IF I your Lord and Master, have washed
your feet, how much more ought you
to wash one another's feet? Hear these
things, all ye nations: give ear, ye that
inhabit the world.

6TH ANTIPHON *John 13: 35*

IN HOC *cognoscent omnes, quia disci-*
puli mei estis, si dilectionem habueritis
ad invicem. Dixit Jesus discipulis suis:
In hoc cognoscent.

BY THIS shall all men know that you
are My disciples, if you have love one
for another: said Jesus to His disciples.
By this shall all men know.

7TH ANTIPHON *I Corinthians 13: 13*

MANEANT *in vobis fides, spes, caritas,*
tria haec: maior autem horum est
caritas. Nunc autem manent fides,
spes, caritas, tria haec: maior horum
est caritas.

LET THESE THREE, faith, hope, and
charity, remain in you; but the greatest of these is charity. And now there
remain faith, hope and charity, these
three; but the greatest of these is charity.

The eighth antiphon is sung with a responsory.

8TH ANTIPHON

℣. CONGREGAVIT NOS *in unum*
Christi amor. Exsultemus et in ipso
iucundemur. Timeamus et amemus
Deum vivum. Et ex corde diligamus
nos sincero.

℣. THE LOVE OF CHRIST has gathered
us together. Let us rejoice in Him and
be glad. Let us fear and love the living
God. And let us love one another with
a sincere heart.

℟. *Ubi caritas et amor, Deus ibi est.*

℟. Where charity and love are, there
is God.

℣. *Simul ergo cum in unum congre-*
gamur: Ne nos mente dividamur,

℣. When, therefore, we are assembled
together: Let us take heed, that we be

not divided in mind. Let malicious quarrels and contentions cease. And let Christ our God dwell among us.
℟. Where charity and love...

℣. Let us also with the blessed see: Thy face in glory, O Christ our God. There to possess immeasurable and happy joy: For infinite ages of ages. Amen.
℟. Where charity and love...

caveamus. Cessent iurgia maligna, cessent lites. Et in medio nostri sit Christus Deus.
℟. *Ubi caritas et amor…*

℣. *Simul quoque cum beatis videamus: Glorianter vultum tuum, Christe Deus: Gaudium, quod est immensum atque probum: Saecula per infinita saeculorum. Amen.* ℟. *Ubi caritas...*

When the ceremony has been completed, the Celebrant prays the Pater Noster *secreto, ending aloud:*

℣. And lead us not into temptation.
℟. But deliver us from evil.
℣. Thou hast commanded Thy commandments, O Lord.
℟. To be exactly observed.
℣. Thou hast washed the feet of Thy disciples.
℟. Despise not the work of Thy hands.

℣. O Lord, hear my prayer.
℟. And let my cry come unto Thee.
℣. The Lord be with you.
℟. And with thy spirit.

℣. *Et ne nos inducas in tentationem.*
℟. *Sed libera nos a malo.*
℣. *Tu mandasti mandata tua, Domine.*
℟. *Custodiri nimis.*
℣. *Tu lavasti pedes discipulorum tuorum.*
℟. *Opera manuum tuarum ne despicias.*

℣. *Domine, exaudi orationem meam.*
℟. *Et clamor meus ad te veniat.*
℣. *Dominus vobiscum.*
℟. *Et cum spiritu tuo.*

COLLECT

BE PRESENT, O Lord, we beseech Thee, at the performance of our service: and since Thou didst vouchsafe to wash the feet of Thy disciples, despise not the work of Thy hands, which Thou hast commanded us to retain: that as here the outward stains are washed away by us and from us, so the inward sins

ADESTO, *Domine, quaesumus, officio servitutis nostrae: et, quia tu discipulis tuis pedes lavare dignatus es, ne despicias opera manuum tuarum, quae nobis retinenda mandasti: ut, sicut hic nobis et a nobis exteriora abluuntur inquinamenta; sic a te omnium nostrum interiora laventur*

peccata. Quod ipse praestare dign-
eris, qui vivis et regnas.

of us all may be blotted out by Thee.
Which do Thou vouchsafe to grant.
Who lives and reigns.

OFFERTORY *Psalm 117: 16-17*

DEXTERA Domini fecit virtutem,
dextera Domini exaltavit me: non
moriar, sed vivam, et narrabo opera
Domini.

THE RIGHT HAND of the Lord hath
wrought strength: the right hand of the
Lord hath exalted me. I shall not die,
but live, and shall declare the works
of the Lord.

SECRET

IPSE TIBI, quaesumus, Domine,
sancte Pater, omnipotens aeterne
Deus, sacrificium nostrum reddat
acceptum, qui discipulis suis in sui
commemorationem hoc fieri hodierna
traditione monstravit, Jesus Christus,
Filius tuus, Dominus noster: Qui
tecum vivit et regnat.

WE BESEECH THEE, O holy Lord,
Father almighty, everlasting God, that
He Himself may render our Sacrifice
acceptable to Thee, Who by the tradi-
tion of today taught His disciples to
do this in remembrance of Him, Jesus
Christ, Thy Son, our Lord, Who with
Thee lives and reigns.

PREFACE OF THE HOLY CROSS *see page 51*

COMMUNION *John 13:12-13, 15*

DOMINUS JESUS, postquam cenavit
cum discipulis suis, lavit pedes eorum,
et ait illis: Scitis quid fecerim vobis
ego, Dominus et Magister? Exemplum
dedi vobis, ut et vos ita faciatis.

THE LORD JESUS, after He had supped
with His disciples, washed their feet,
and said to them: Know you what I,
your Lord and Master, have done to
you? I gave you an example, that you
also may do likewise.

POSTCOMMUNION

REFECTI vitalibus alimentis, quaesu-
mus, Domine Deus noster: ut quod
tempore nostrae mortalitatis exse-
quimur, immortalitatis tuae munere
consequamur. Per Dominum nostrum.

STRENGTHENED with life-giving Food,
we beseech Thee, O Lord, our God,
that what we do in our mortal life may
bring us to the reward of life immortal
with Thee. Through our Lord.

Benedicamus Domino *is sung instead of* Ite missa est *and ends the Mass.*

PROCESSION TO THE ALTAR OF REPOSE

Accompanied by the sacred ministers, the Celebrant carries the Blessed Sacrament to the Altar of Repose where it will remain until the Mass of the Presanctified on Good Friday, when no consecration takes place. During the procession the hymn Pange Lingua Gloriosi Corporis *is sung unto the strophe* Tantum Ergo. *See page 126.*

S ING, my tongue, the Savior's glory:
Of His Flesh the mystery sing;
Of His Blood all price exceeding.
Shed by our immortal King.
Destined for the world's redemption
From a noble womb to spring.

PANGE, lingua, gloriosi
Corporis mysterium,
Sanguinisque pretiosi,
quem in mundi pretium
fructus ventris generosi
Rex effudit Gentium.

Of a pure and spotless Virgin,
Born for us on earth below,
He, as Man with man conversing,
Stayed the seeds of truth to sow,
Then He closed in solemn order
Wondrously His life of woe.

Nobis datus, nobis natus
ex intacta Virgine,
et in mundo conversatus,
sparso verbi semine,
sui moras incolatus
miro clausit ordine.

On the night of His last supper,
Seated with His chosen band,
He, the Paschal Victim eating,
First fulfills the Law's command;
Then as food to all His brethren
Gives Himself with His own hand.

In supremae nocte cenae
recumbens cum fratribus
observata lege plene
cibis in legalibus,
cibum turbae duodenae
se dat suis manibus.

Word made Flesh, the bread of nature,
By His words to Flesh He turns;
Wine into His Blood He changes:
What though sense no change
   discerns,
Only be the heart in earnest,
Faith her lesson quickly learns.

Verbum caro, panem verum
verbo carnem efficit:
fitque sanguis Christi merum,
et si sensus deficit,
ad firmandum cor sincerum
sola fides sufficit.

The ciborium is placed on the Altar of Repose, and after being incensed is placed in the tabernacle. Meanwhile Tantum Ergo *is sung.*

TANTUM ERGO Sacramentum
veneremur cernui:
et antiquum documentum
novo cedat ritui:
praestet fides supplementum
sensuum defectui.

Genitori, Genitoque
laus et iubilatio,
salus, honor, virtus quoque
sit et benedictio:
procedenti ab utroque
compar sit laudatio. Amen.

D OWN IN ADORATION falling,
Lo, the Sacred Host we hail,
Lo, o'er ancient forms departing
Newer rites of grace prevail;
Faith for all defects supplying,
Where the feeble senses fail.

To the everlasting Father
And the Son who reigns on high
With the Holy Ghost proceeding
Forth from each eternally,
Be salvation, honor, blessing,
Might and endless majesty. Amen.

THE STRIPPING OF THE ALTARS

The Celebrant intones in a clear voice verse 19 of Psalm 21.

℣. DIVIDUNT *sibi indumenta mea, et de veste mea mittunt sortem.*

℣. THEY PARTED My garments amongst them, and upon My vesture they cast lots.

He then pronounces the opening verse and the choir or sacred ministers take up the psalm.

PSALM 21

DEUS MEUS, Deus meus, quare me dereliquísti? Longe abes a précibus, a verbis clamóris mei. Deus meus, clamo per diem, et non exáudis, et nocte, et non atténdis ad me. Tu autem in sanctuário hábitas, laus Israël. In te speravérunt patres nostri, speravérunt et liberásti eos. Ad te clamavérunt et salvi facti sunt, in te speravérunt et non sunt confúsi. Ego autem sum vermis et non homo oppróbrium hóminum et despéctio plebis. Omnes vidéntes me derídent me, didúcunt lábia, ágitant caput: Confídit in Dómino: líberet

MY GOD, my God, look upon me: why hast Thou forsaken me? Far from my salvation are the words of my sins. O my God, I shall cry by day and Thou wilt not hear: and by night, and it shall not be reputed as folly in me. But Thou dwellest in the holy place, O Thou Praise of Israel. In Thee our fathers have hoped: they have hoped, and Thou hast delivered them. They cried unto Thee, and were delivered: they trusted in Thee, and were not confounded. But I am a worm and no man: a reproach of men, and the outcast of the people. All they that saw me have laughed me to scorn: they have spoken with the lips, and wagged their head. He trusted the Lord, let Him rescue him: let Him deliver him, seeing He delighteth in him. For Thou art He that hast drawn me out of the womb: my hope from the breasts of my mother. I was cast upon Thee from the womb. From my mother's womb thou art my God: depart not from me. For tribulation is very near; for there is none to help me. Many calves have surrounded me: fat bulls have besieged me. They gaped upon me with their mouths, as a ravening and a roaring lion. I am poured out like water, and all my bones are scattered. My heart is like melting wax in the midst of my bowels. My strength is dried up like a potsherd, and my tongue cleaveth to my jaws: and Thou hast brought me into the dust of death. For many dogs have compassed me: the council of the malignant have besieged me. They pierced my hands and my feet: they have numbered all my bones. They look and stare upon me. They part my garments among them, and upon my vesture do they cast lots. But Thou, O Lord, remove not Thy help to a distance from me: look towards my defense. O God, deliver my soul from the sword: my darling from the power

eum, erípiat eum, si díligit eum. Tu útique duxísti me inde ab útero; secúrum me fecísti ad úbera matris meæ. Tibi tráditus sum inde ab ortu, ab útero matris meæ Deus meus es tu. Ne longe stéteris a me, quóniam tríbulor; prope esto: quia non est adjútor. Circúmstant me juvénci multi, tauri Basan cingunt me. Apériunt contra me os suum, sicut leo vapax et rúgiens. Sicut aqua effúsus sum, et disjúncta sunt ómnia ossa mea: Factum est cor meum tamquam cera, liquéscit in viscéribus meis. Aruit tamquam testa guttur meum, et lingua mea adhaéret fáucibus meis, et in púlverem mortis deduxísti me. Étenim circúmstant me canes multi, catérva male agéntium cingit me. Fodérunt manus meas et pedes meos, dinumeráre possum ómnia ossa mea. Ipsi vero aspíciunt et vidéntes me lætántur; dívidunt sibi induménta mea, et de veste mea mittunt sortem. Tu autem, Dómine, ne longe stéteris: auxílium meum, ad juvándum me festína. Éripe a gládio ánimam meam, et de manu canis vitam meam; Salva me ex ore leónis et me míserum a córnibus bubalórum. Enarrábo nomen tuum frátribus meis, in médio cœtu laudábo te. Qui timétis Dóminum, laudáte eum: univérsum semen Jacob, celebrate eum; timéte eum, omne semen Israël. Neque enim sprevit nec fastidívit misériam míseri:

neque abscóndit fáciem suam ab eo et, dum clamávit ad eum, audívit eum. A te venit laudátio mea in cœtu magno, vota mea reddam in conspéctu timéntium eum. Edent páuperes et saturabúntur; laudábunt Dóminum, qui quaérunt eum: vivant corda vestra in saécula. Recordabúntur et converténtur ad Dóminum univérsi fines terræ; Et procúmbent in conspéctu ejus univérsæ famíliæ géntium, Quóniam Dómini est regnum, et ipse dominátur in géntibus. Eum solum adorábunt omnes qui dórmiunt in terra, coram eo curvabúntur omnes, qui descéndunt in púlverem. Et ánima mea ipsi vivet, semen meum sérviet ei, Narrábit de Dómino generatióni ventúræ, et annuntiábunt justítiam ejus pópulo, qui nascétur: Hæc fecit Dóminus.

of the dog! Save me from the lion's mouth: and my affliction from the horns of the unicorns. I will declare Thy Name unto my brethren: in the midst of the church will I praise Thee. Ye that fear the Lord, praise Him: all ye seed of Jacob, glorify Him. Let all the seed of Israel fear Him. Because He hath not slighted nor despised the supplication of the poor man. Neither hath He hid His face from me: but when I cried unto Him, He heard me. With Thee is my praise in the great church: I will pay my vows in the sight of them that fear Him. The poor shall eat and be filled, and they shall praise the Lord that seek Him: their hearts shall live for ever and ever. All the ends of the earth shall remember and turn unto the Lord. And all the kindred of the Gentiles shall adore in His sight. For the kingdom is the Lord's: and He shall have dominion over the nations. All the fat ones of the earth have eaten and have adored: all they that go down to the earth shall fall before Him. My soul also shall live unto Him: and my seed shall serve Him. The generation to come shall tell it unto the Lord: and the heavens shall declare His righteousness unto a people that shall be born, whom the Lord hath made.

After all the altars have been stripped, the Celebrant repeats the Antiphon Dividunt sibi *before returning to the sacristy. It is customary for adoration of the Blessed Sacrament to continue until midnight.*

GOOD FRIDAY

Black and Violet　　　　　　　　　　　　　　　　　　*First Class*

≈ *Mass of the Presanctified* ≈

1ST COLLECT

O GOD, Who by the Passion of Thy Christ, our Lord, hast loosened the bonds of death, that heritage of the first sin to which all men of later times did succeed: make us so conformed to Him that, as we must needs have borne the likeness of earthly nature, so we may by sanctification bear the likeness of heavenly grace. Through the same Christ our Lord.

DEUS, qui peccáti véteris hereditárium mortem, in qua posteritátis genus omne succésserat, Christi tui, Dómini nostri, passióne solvísti: da, ut, confórmes eídem facti; sicut imáginem terrénæ natúræ necessitáte portávimus, ita imáginem cæléstis grátiæ sanctificatióne portémus. Per eúmdem Christum Dóminum nostrum.

1ST EPISTLE *Osee 6: 1-6*

THUS SAITH THE LORD: In their affliction they will rise early to Me: Come, and let us return to the Lord, for He hath taken us, and He will heal us, He will strike, and He will cure us. He will revive us after two days: on the third day He will raise us up and we shall live in His sight. We shall know and we shall follow on, that we may know the Lord. His going forth is prepared as the morning light and He will come to us as the early and the latter rain to the earth. What shall I do to thee, O Ephraim? What shall I do to thee, O Juda? Your mercy is as a morning cloud and as the dew that goeth away in the morning. For this reason

HÆC DICIT DÓMINUS: In tribulatióne sua mane consúrgent ad me: Veníte, et revertámur ad Dóminum: quia ipse cepit, et sanábit nos: percútiet, et curábit nos. Vivificábit nos post duos dies: in die tértia suscitábit nos, et vivémus in conspéctu ejus. Sciémus, sequemúrque, ut cognoscámus Dóminum: quasi dilúculum præparátus est egréssus ejus, et véniet quasi imber nobis temporáneus, et serótinus terræ. Quid fáciam tibi Ephraim? Quid fáciam tibi Juda? Misericórdia vestra quasi nubes matutína, et quasi ros mane pertránsiens. Propter hoc dolávi in prophétis, occídi eos in verbis oris mei: et judícia tua quasi lux egrediéntur. Quia misericórdiam volui, et non sacrifícium, et sciéntiam Dei plus quam holocáusta.

have I hewed them by the Prophets, I have slain them by the words of My mouth: and Thy judgments shall go forth as the light. For I desired mercy and not sacrifice: and the knowledge of God more than holocausts.

RESPONSORY *Habakkuk 3: 2, 3*

DÓMINE, *audívi audíum tuum, et tímui: considerávi ópera tua, et expávi. In médio duórum animálium innotescéris: dum appropinquáverint anni cognoscéris: dum advénerit, tempus, ostendéris. In eo, dum conturbáta fúerit ánima mea: in ira, misericórdiæ memor eris. Deus a Líbano véniet, et Sanctus de monte umbróso, et condénso. Opéruit cælos majéstas ejus: et laudis ejus plena est terra.*

O LORD, I have heard Thy hearing and was afraid: I have considered Thy works and trembled. In the midst of two animals Thou shalt be made known: when the years shall draw nigh Thou shalt be known: when the time shall come, Thou shalt be manifested. When my soul shall be in trouble, Thou wilt remember mercy, even in Thy wrath. God will come from Libanus, and the Holy One from the shady and thickly covered mountain. His majesty covered the heavens: and the earth is full of His praise.

2ND COLLECT

S. *Orémus.*

℣. *Flectámus genua.*

℟. *Leváte.*

S. Let us pray.

℣. Let us kneel down.

℟. Arise.

DEUS, *a quo et Judas reátus sui pœnam, et confessiónis suæ latro præmium sumpsit, concéde nobis tuæ propitiatiónis efféctum: ut sicut in passióne sua Jesus Christus Dóminus noster divérsa utrísque íntulit stipéndia meritórum; ita nobis, abláto vetustátis erróre, resurrectiónis suæ*

O GOD, from Whom Judas received the punishment of his guilt, and the thief the reward of his confession: grant unto us the full fruit of Thy clemency; that even as in His Passion, our Lord Jesus Christ gave to each a retribution according to his merits, so having taken away our old sins, He may bestow upon us the grace of His Resurrection. Who with Thee lives and reigns.

grátiam largiátur: Qui técum vivit et regnat.

2ND EPISTLE *Exodus 12: 1-11*

IN THOSE DAYS the Lord said to Moses and Aaron in the land of Egypt: This month shall be to you the beginning of months: it shall be the first in the months of the year. Speak ye to the whole assembly of the children of Israel, and say to them: On the tenth day of this month let every man take a lamb by their families and houses. But if the number be less than may suffice to eat the lamb, he shall take unto him his neighbor that joineth to his house, according to the number of souls which may be enough to eat the lamb. And it shall be a lamb without blemish, a male, of one year: according to which rite also you shall take a kid. And you shall keep it until the fourteenth day of this month: and the whole multitude of the children of Israel shall sacrifice it in the evening. And they shall take of blood thereof, and put it upon both the side posts, and on the upper door posts of the houses, wherein they shall eat it. And they shall eat the flesh that night roasted at the fire: and unleavened bread with wild lettuce. You shall not eat thereof anything raw, nor boiled in water, but only roasted at the fire. You shall eat the head with the feet and entrails thereof. Neither shall there remain anything of

IN DIÉBUS ILLIS: Dixit Dóminus ad Móysen et Aaron in terra Ægypti: Mensis iste, vobis princípium ménsium: primus erit in ménsibus anni. Loquímini ad univérsum cœtum filiórum Israël, et dícite eis: Décima die mensis hujus tollat unusquísque agnum per famílias et domos suas. Sin autem minor est númerus, ut suffícere possit ad vescéndum agnum, assúmet vicínum suum qui junctus est dómui suæ, juxta númerum animárum quæ suffícere possunt ad esum agni. Erit autem agnus absque mácula, másculus, annículus: juxta quem ritum tollétis et hædum. Et servábitis eum usque ad quartamdécimam diem mensis hujus: immolabítque eum univérsa multitúdo filiórum Israël ad vésperam. Et sument de sánguine ejus, ac ponent super utrúmque postem, et in superlimináribus domórum, in quíbus cómedent illum. Et edent carnes nocte illa assas igni, et ázymos panes cum lactúcis agréstibus. Non comedétis ex eo crudum quid, nec coctum aqua, sed tantum assum igni: caput cum pédibus ejus et intestínis vorábitis. Nec remanébit quídquam ex eo usque mane. Si quid residuum fúerit, igne comburétis. Sic autem comedétis illum: Renes vestros accingétis, et calceaménta habébitis in pédibus, tenéntes báculos in mánibus, et comedétis festinánter: est enim Phase (id est tránsitus) Dómini.

it until morning. If there be a thing left, you shall burn it with fire. And thus you shall eat it: You shall gird your reins, and you shall have shoes on your feet, holding staves in your hands, and you shall eat in haste; for it is the Phase (that is the Passage) of the Lord.

RESPONSORY *Psalm 139: 2-10, 14*

ÉRIPE ME, Dómine, ab hómine malo: a viro iníquo líbera me. Qui cogitavérunt malítias in corde: tota die constituébant praélia. Acuérunt linguas suas sicut serpéntes: venénum áspidum sub lábiis eórum. Custódi me, Dómine, de manu peccatóris: et ab homínibus iníquis líbera me. Qui cogitavérunt supplantáre gressus meos: abscondérunt supérbi láqueum mihi. Et funes extendérunt in láqueum pédibus meis: juxta iter scándalum posuérunt mihi. Dixi Dómino: Deus meus es tu: exáudi, Dómine, vocem oratiónis meæ. Dómine, Dómine, virtus salútis meæ: obúmbra caput meum in die belli. Ne tradas me a desidério meo peccatóri: cogitavérunt advérsus me: ne derelínquas me, ne umquam exalténtur. Caput circúitus eórum: labor labiórum ipsórum opériet eos. Verúmtamen justi confitebúntur nómini tuo: et habitábunt recti cum vulto tuo.

DELIVER ME, O Lord, from the evil man: rescue me from the unjust man. Who have devised iniquities in their hearts: all the day long they designed battles. They have sharpened their tongues like a serpent; the venom of asps is under their lips. Keep me, O Lord, from the hand of the wicked: and from unjust men deliver me. Who have proposed to supplant my steps. The proud have hidden a net for me. And they have stretched out cords for a snare for my feet; they have laid for me a stumbling block by the wayside. I said to the Lord: Thou art my God. Hear, O Lord, the voice of my supplication. O Lord, Lord, the strength of my salvation: overshadow my head in the day of battle. Give me not up from my desire to the wicked: they have plotted against me. Do not Thou forsake me, lest at any time they should triumph. The head of them compassing me about: the labor of their lips shall overwhelm them. But the just shall give glory to Thy Name: and the upright shall dwell with Thy countenance.

ILLUSTRATION BY DANIEL MITSUI

THE PASSION OF OUR LORD JESUS CHRIST
ACCORDING TO ST. JOHN

AT THAT TIME Jesus went forth with His disciples over the brook Cedron, where there was a garden, into which He entered with His disciples. And Judas also, who betrayed Him, knew the place: because Jesus had often resorted thither together with His disciples. Judas therefore having received a band of soldiers and servants from the chief priests and the Pharisees, cometh thither with lanterns and torches and weapons. Jesus therefore, knowing that all things that should come upon Him, went forth and said to them: ✠ Whom seek ye? They answered Him: Jesus of Nazareth. Jesus saith to them: ✠ I am He. And Judas also, who betrayed Him, stood with them. As soon therefore as He had said to them: ✠ I am He; they went backward

IN ILLO TÉMPORE: Egréssus est Jesus cum discípulis suis trans torréntem Cedron, ubi erat hortus, in quem introívit ipse, et discípuli ejus. Sciébat autem et Judas, qui tradébat eum, locum: quia frequénter Jesus convénerat illuc cum discípulis suis. Judas ergo, cum accepísset cohórtem, et a pontifícibus et pharisaéis minístros, venit illuc cum latérnis, et fácibus, et armis. Jesus ítaque sciens ómnia, quæ ventúra erant super eum, procéssit, et dixit eis: ✠ Quem quaéritis? Respondérunt ei: Jesum Nazarénum. Dicit eis Jesus: ✠ Ego sum. Stabat autem et Judas, qui tradébat eum, cum ipsis. Ut ergo dixit eis: ✠ Ego sum: abiérunt retrórsum, et cecidérunt in terram. Íterum ergo interrogávit eos: ✠ Quem quaéritis?

Illi autem dixérunt: Jesum Nazarénum. Respóndit Jesus: ✠ *Dixi vobis, quia ego sum: si ergo me quaéritis, sínite hos abíre. Ut implerétur sermo, quem dixit: Quia quos dedísti mihi, non pérdidi ex eis quemquam. Simon ergo Petrus habens gládium edúxit eum: et percússit pontíficis servum: et abscídit aurículam ejus déxteram. Erat autem nomen servo Malchus. Dixit ergo Jesus Petro:* ✠ *Mitte gládium tuum in vagínam. Cálicem, quem dedit mihi Pater, non bibam illum? Cohors ergo, et tribúnus, et minístri Judæórum comprehendérunt Jesum, et ligavérunt eum. Et adduxérunt eum ad Annam primum, erat enim socer Cáiphæ, qui erat póntifex anni illíus.Erat autem Cáiphas, qui consílium déderat Judáeis: Quia éxpedit unum hóminem mori pro pópulo. Sequebátur autem Jesum Simon Petrus, et álius discípulus. Discípulus autem ille erat notus pontífici, et introívit cum Jesu in átrium pontíficis. Petrus autem stabat ad óstium foris. Exívit ergo discípulus álius, qui erat notus pontífici, et dixit ostiáriæ: et introdúxit Petrum. Dicit ergo Petro ancílla ostiária: Numquid et tu ex discípulis es hóminis istíus? Dicit ille: Non sum. Stabant autem servi et minístri ad prunas, quia frigus erat, et calefaciébant se: erat autem cum eis et Petrus stans, et calefáciens se.Póntifex ergo interrogávit Jesum de*

and fell to the ground. Again therefore He asked them: ✠ Whom seek ye? And they said: Jesus of Nazareth. Jesus answered: ✠ I have told you that I am He. If therefore you seek Me, let these go their way. That the word might be fulfilled which He said: Of them whom Thou hast given Me, I have not lost anyone. Then Simon Peter, having a sword, drew it and struck the servant of the high priest and cut off his right ear. And the name of the servant was Malchus. Jesus therefore said to Peter: ✠ Put up thy sword in the scabbard. The chalice which My Father hath given Me, shall I not drink it? Then the band and the tribune and the servants of the Jews took Jesus, and bound Him. And they led Him away to Annas first, for he was father-in-law to Caiphas, who was the high priest that year. Now Caiphas was he who had given the counsel to the Jews: that it was expedient that one man should die for the people. And Simon Peter followed Jesus: and so did another disciple. And that disciple was known to the high priest and went in with Jesus into the court of the high priest. But Peter stood at the door without. The other disciple therefore, who was known to the high priest, went out and spoke to the portress and brought in Peter. The maid therefore that was portress saith to Peter: Art not thou also one of this man's disciples?

He saith: I am not. Now the servants and ministers stood at a fire of coals, because it was cold, and warmed themselves. And with them was Peter, also, standing and warming himself. The high priest therefore asked Jesus of His disciples and of His doctrine. Jesus answered him: ✠ I have spoken openly to the world. I have always taught in the synagogue and in the temple, whither all the Jews resort: and in secret I have spoken nothing. Why asketh thou Me? Ask them who have heard what I have spoken unto them. Behold they know what things I have said. And when He had said these things, one of the servants, standing by, gave Jesus a blow, saying: Answerest Thou the high priest so? Jesus answered him: ✠ If I have spoken evil, give testimony of the evil; but if well, why strikest thou Me? And Annas sent Him bound to Caiphas the high priest. And Simon Peter was standing and warming himself. They said therefore to him: Art not thou also one of His disciples? He denied it and said: I am not. One of the servants of the high priest (a kinsman to him whose ear Peter cut off) saith to him: Did I not see thee in the garden with Him? Again therefore Peter denied; and immediately the cock crowed. Then they led Jesus from Caiphas to the governor's hall. And it was morning; and they went not into the hall, that they might not be defiled,

discípulis suis, et de doctrína ejus. Respóndit ei Jesus: ✠ Ego palam locútus sum mundo: ego semper dócui in synagóga et in templo, quo omnes Judaéi convéniunt: et in occúlto locútus sum nihil. Quid me intérrogas? intérroga eos, qui audiérunt quid locutus sim ipsis: ecce hi sciunt quæ díxerim ego. Hæc autem cum dixísset, unus assístens ministrórum dedit álapam Jesu, dicens: Sic respóndes pontífici? Respóndit ei Jesus: ✠ Si male locútus sum, testimónium pérhibe de malo: si autem bene, quid me cædis? Et misit eum Annas ligátum ad Cáipham pontíficem. Erat autem Simon Petrus stans, et calefáciens se. Dixérunt ergo ei: Numquid et tu ex discípulis ejus es? Negávit ille, et dixit: Non sum. Dicit ei unus ex servis pontíficis, cognátus ejus, cujus abscídit Petrus aurículam: Nonne ego te vidi in horto cum illo? Íterum ergo negávit Petrus: et statim gallus cantávit. Addúcunt ergo Jesum a Cáipha in prætórium. Erat autem mane: et ipsi non introiérunt in prætórium, ut non contaminaréntur, sed ut manducárent Pascha. Exívit ergo Pilátus ad eos foras, et dixit: Quam accusatiónem affértis advérsus hóminem hunc? Respondérunt, et dixérunt ei: Si non esset hic malefáctor, non tibi tradidissémus eum. Dixit ergo eis Pilátus: Accípite eum vos, et secúndum legem vestram judicáte eum.

Dixérunt ergo ei Judaéi: Nobis non licet interfícere quemquam. Ut sermo Jesu implerétur, quem dixit, significans qua morte esset moritúrus. Introívit ergo íterum in prætórium Pilátus, et vocávit Jesum, et dixit ei: Tu es Rex Judæórum? Respóndit Jesus: ✠ A temetípso hoc dicis, an álii dixérunt tibi de me? Respóndit Pilátus: Numquid ego Judaéus sum? Gens tua et pontífices tradidérunt te mihi: quid fecísti? Respóndit Jesus: ✠ Regnum meum non est de hoc mundo. Si ex hoc mundo esset regnum meum, minístri mei útique decertárent ut non tráderer Judaéis: nunc autem regnum meum non est hinc. Dixit ítaque ei Pilátus: Ergo rex es tu? Respóndit Jesus: ✠ Tu dicis, quia Rex sum ego. Ego in hoc natus sum, et ad hoc veni in mundum, ut testimónium perhíbeam veritáti: omnis qui est ex veritáte, audit vocem meam. Dicit ei Pilátus: Quid est véritas? Et cum hoc dixísset, íterum exívit ad Judaéos, et dicit eis: Ego nullam invénio in eo causam. Est autem consuetúdo vobis ut unum dimíttam vobis in Pascha: vultis ergo dimíttam vobis Regem Judæórum? Clamavérunt ergo rursum omnes, dicéntes: Non hunc, sed Barábbam. Erat autem Barábbas latro. Tunc ergo apprehéndit Pilátus Jesum, et flagellávit. Et mílites plecténtes corónam de spinis, imposuérunt cápiti ejus: et veste purpúrea circumdedérunt

but that they might eat the Pasch. Pilate therefore went out to them, and said: What accusation bring you against this man? They answered and said to him: If He were not a malefactor, we would not have delivered Him up to thee. Pilate therefore said to them: Take Him you, and judge Him according to your law. The Jews therefore said to him: It is not lawful for us to put any man to death. That the word of Jesus might be fulfilled, which He said, signifying what death He should die. Pilate therefore went into the hall again and called Jesus and said to Him: Art Thou the King of the Jews? Jesus answered: ✠ Sayest thou this thing of thyself, or have other told it thee of Me? Pilate answered: Am I a Jew? Thine own nation and the chief priests have delivered Thee up to me. What hast Thou done? Jesus answered: ✠ My kingdom is not of this world. If My kingdom were of this world, My servants would certainly strive that I should not be delivered to the Jews: but now My kingdom is not from hence. Pilate therefore said to Him: Art Thou a king then? Jesus answered: ✠ Thou sayest I am a king. For this was I born, and for this came I into the world; that I should give testimony of the truth. Every one that is of the truth heareth My voice. Pilate saith to Him: What is truth? And when he had said this, he went out again to the Jews and saith to them: I find no cause in Him. But you have a custom that I should release one unto you at the Pasch. Will you, therefore, that I release unto you the King of the Jews? Then cried they all again, saying: Not this man, but Barabbas. Now Barabbas was a robber. Then therefore Pilate took Jesus and scourged Him. And the soldiers plaiting a crown of thorns, put it upon His head; and they put on Him a purple garment. And they came to Him and said: Hail, King of the Jews. And they gave Him blows. Pilate therefore went forth again and saith to them: Behold, I bring Him forth unto you, that you may know that I find no cause in Him. (Jesus therefore came forth, bearing the crown of thorns and the purple garment.) And he saith to them: Behold the man. When the chief priests, therefore, and the servants had seen Him, they cried out, saying: Crucify Him, crucify Him. Pilate saith to them: Take Him you, and crucify Him; for I find no cause in Him. The Jews answered him: We have a law, and according to the law He ought to die, because He made Himself the Son of God. When Pilate, therefore, had heard this saying, he feared the more. And he entered into the hall again; and he said to Jesus: Whence art Thou? But Jesus gave him no answer. Pilate therefore saith to Him: Speakest Thou not to me? Knowest Thou not that I have power to crucify

eum. Et veniébant ad eum, et dicébant: Ave, Rex Judæórum. Et dabant ei álapas. Exívit ergo íterum Pilátus foras, et dicit eis: Ecce addúco vobis eum foras, ut cognoscátis, quia nullam invénio in eo causam. (Exívit ergo Jesus portans corónam spíneam, et purpúreum vestiméntum.) Et dicit eis: Ecce homo. Cum ergo vidíssent eum pontífices et minístri, clamábant, dicéntes: Crucifíge, crucifíge eum. Dicit eis Pilátus: Accípite eum vos, et crucifígite: ego enim non invénio in eo causam. Respondérunt ei Judæi: Nos legem habémus, et secúndum legem debet mori, quia Fílium Dei se fecit. Cum ergo audísset Pilátus hunc sermónem, magis tímuit. Et ingréssus est prætórium íterum: et dixit ad Jesum: Unde es tu? Jesus autem respónsum non dedit ei. Dicit ergo ei Pilátus: Mihi non lóqueris? nescis quia potestátem hábeo crucifígere te, et potestátem hábeo dimíttere te? Respóndit Jesus: ✠ Non habéres potestátem advérsum me ullam, nisi tibi datum esset désuper. Proptérea, qui me trádidit tibi, majus peccátum habet. Et exínde quærébat Pilátus dimíttere eum. Judæi autem clamábant dicéntes: Si hunc dimíttis, non es amícus Caésaris. Omnis enim, qui se regem facit, contradícit Caésari. Pilátus autem cum audísset hos sermónes, addúxit foras Jesum, et sedit pro tribunáli, in loco qui dícitur Lithóstrotos, hebráice autem Gábbatha. Erat autem Parascéve Paschæ, hora quasi sexta, et dicit Judaéis: Ecce Rex vester. Illi autem clamábant: Tolle, tolle, crucifíge eum. Dicit eis Pilátus: Regem vestrum crucifígam? Respondérunt pontífices: Non habémus regem, nisi Caésarem. Tunc ergo trádidit eis illum ut crucifigerétur. Suscepérunt autem Jesum, et eduxérunt. Et bájulans sibi crucem, exívit in eum, qui dícitur Calváriæ locum, hebráice autem Gólgotha: ubi crucifixérunt eum, et cum eo álios duos, hinc et hinc, médium autem Jesum. Scripsit autem et títulum Pilátus: et pósuit super crucem. Erat autem scriptum: Jesus Nazarénus, Rex Judæórum. Hunc ergo títulum multi Judæórum legérunt, quia prope civitátem erat locus, ubi crucifíxus est Jesus. Et erat scriptum hebráice, græce, et latíne. Dicébant ergo Piláto pontífices Judæórum: Noli scríbere, Rex Judæórum, sed quia ipse dixit: Rex sum Judæórum. Respóndit Pilátus: Quod scripsi, scripsi. Mílites ergo cum crucifixíssent eum, accepérunt vestiménta ejus (et fecérunt quátuor partes: unicuíque míliti partem), et túnicam. Erat autem túnica inconsútilis, désuper contéxta per totum. Dixérunt ergo ad ínvicem: Non scindámus eam, sed sortiámur de illa cujus sit. Ut Scriptúra implerétur, dicens: Partíti sunt vestiménta mea sibi: et in vestem meam misérunt sortem. Et mílites quidem

Thee, and I have power to release Thee? Jesus answered: ✠ Thou shouldst not have any power against Me, unless it were given thee from above. Therefore, he that hath delivered Me to thee hath a greater sin. And from henceforth Pilate sought to release Him. But the Jews cried out, saying: If thou release this man, thou art not Caesar's friend. For whosoever maketh himself a king speaketh against Caesar. Now when Pilate had heard these words, he brought Jesus forth and sat down in the judgment seat, in the place that is called Lithostrotos, and in Hebrew Gabbatha. And it was Parasceve of the Pasch, about the sixth hour; and he saith to the Jews: Behold your King. But they cried out: Away with Him. Away with Him. Crucify Him. Pilate saith to them: Shall I crucify your King? The chief priests answered: We have no king but Caesar. Then, therefore, he delivered Him to them to be crucified. And they took Jesus and led Him forth. And bearing His cross, He went forth to that place, which is called Calvary but in Hebrew Golgotha; where they crucified Him, and with Him two others, one on each side and Jesus in the midst. And Pilate wrote a title also: and he put it upon the cross. And the writing was: Jesus of Nazareth, the King of the Jews. This title therefore many of the Jews did read: because the place where Jesus was crucified was nigh to the city. And it was written in Hebrew, Greek and in Latin. Then the chief priests of the Jews said to Pilate: Write not: The King of the Jews; but that He said: I am the King of the Jews. Pilate answered: What I have written, I have written. The soldiers therefore, when they had crucified Him, took His garments (and they made four parts, to every soldier a part) and also His coat. Now the coat was without seam, woven from the top throughout. They said then one to another: Let us not cut it, but let us cast lots for it, whose it shall be: that the Scripture might be fulfilled which saith: They have parted My garments among them, and upon My vesture they have cast lots. And the soldiers indeed did these things. Now there stood by the cross of Jesus His Mother, and His Mother's sister, Mary of Cleophas, and Mary Magdalen. When Jesus therefore had seen His Mother and the disciple standing whom He loved, He saith to His Mother: ✠ Woman, behold thy son. After that, He saith to the disciple: ✠ Behold thy Mother. And from that hour, the disciple took her to his own. Afterwards, Jesus, knowing that all things were now accomplished, that the Scripture might be fulfilled, said: ✠ I thirst. Now there was a vessel set there, full of vinegar. And they, putting a sponge full of vinegar and hyssop, put it to His mouth. Jesus

hæc fecérunt. Stabant autem juxta crucem Jesu, mater ejus, et soror matris ejus María Cléophæ, et María Magdaléne. Cum vidísset ergo Jesus matrem, et discípulum stantem quem diligébat, dicit matri suæ: ✠ *Múlier, ecce fílius tuus. Deínde dicit discípulo:* ✠ *Ecce mater tua. Et ex illa hora accépit eam discípulus in sua. Póstea sciens Jesus quia ómnia consummáta sunt, ut consummarétur Scriptúra, dixit:* ✠ *Sítio. Vas ergo erat pósitum acéto plenum. Illi autem spóngiam plenam acéto, hyssópo circumponéntes, obtulérunt ori ejus. Cum ergo accepísset Jesus acétum, dixit:* ✠ *Consummátum est. Et inclináto cápite trádidit spíritum. Judaéi ergo (quóniam Parascéve erat) ut non remanérent in cruce córpora sábbato (erat enim magnus dies ille sábbati) rogavérunt Pilátum, ut frangeréntur eórum crura, et tolleréntur. Venérunt ergo mílites: et primi quidem fregérunt crura, et altérius, qui crucifíxus est cum eo. Ad Jesum autem cum veníssent, ut vidérunt eum jam mórtuum, non fregérunt ejus crura, sed unus mílitum láncea latus ejus apéruit, et contínuo exívit sanguis, et aqua. Et qui vidit, testimónium perhíbuit: et verum est testimónium ejus. Et ille scit, quia vera dicit: ut et vos credátis. Facta sunt enim hæc, ut Scriptúra implerétur: Os non comminuétis ex eo. Et íterum ália Scriptúra dicit: Vidébunt in quem transfixérunt. Post hæc autem rogávit Pilátum Joseph ab Arimathaéa (eo quod esset discípulus Jesu, occúltus autem propter metum Judæórum) ut tólleret corpus Jesu. Et permísit Pilátus. Venit ergo, et tulit corpus Jesu. Venit autem et Nicodémus, qui venérat ad Jesum nocte primum, ferens mixtúram myrrhæ, et áloës, quasi libras centum. Accepérunt ergo corpus Jesu, et ligavérunt illud línteis cum aromátibus, sicut mos est Judæis sepelíre. Erat autem in loco, ubi crucifíxus est, hortus: et in horto monuméntum novum, in quo nondum quisquam pósitus erat. Ibi ergo propter Parascéven Judæórum, quia juxta erat monuméntum, posuérunt Jesum.*

therefore, when He had taken the vinegar, said: ✛ It is consummated. And bowing His head, He gave up the ghost. KNEEL AND PAUSE Then the Jews (because it was the Parasceve), that the bodies might not remain upon the cross on the Sabbath day (for that was a great Sabbath day), besought Pilate that their legs might be broken and that they might be taken away. The soldiers therefore came, and they broke the legs of the first, and of the other that was crucified with Him. But after they were come to Jesus, when they saw that He was already dead, they did not break His legs. But one of the soldiers with a spear opened His side, and immediately there came out blood and water. And he that saw it hath given testimony: and his testimony is true. And he knoweth that he saith true: that you also may believe. For these things were done that the Scripture might be fulfilled: you shall not break a bone of Him. And again another Scripture saith: They shall look on Him whom they pierced. And after these things, Joseph of Arimathea (because he was a disciple of Jesus, but secretly for fear of the Jews) besought Pilate that he might take away the Body of Jesus. And Pilate gave leave. He came therefore and took away the Body of Jesus. And Nicodemus also came (he who at the first came to Jesus by night), bringing a mixture of myrrh and aloes, about a hundred pound weight. They took therefore the Body of Jesus and bound it in linen cloths, with the spices, as the manner of the Jews is to bury. Now there was in the place where He was crucified a garden: and in the garden a new sepulcher, wherein no man yet had been laid. There, therefore, because of the Parasceve of the Jews, they laid Jesus, because the sepulcher was nigh at hand.

THE GREAT INTERCESSIONS

FOR HOLY CHURCH

LET US PRAY, dearly beloved, for the holy Church of God: that our Lord and God may deign to give it peace, keep it in unity, and guard it throughout the world, subjecting to it principalities and powers: and may grant unto us that, leading a peaceful and quiet life, we may glorify God, the Father almighty.

ORÉMUS, dilectíssimi nobis, pro Ecclésia sancta Dei: ut eam Deus et Dóminus noster pacificáre, adunáre, et custodíre dignétur toto orbe terrárum: subjíciens ei principátus, et potestátes: detque nobis quiétam et tranquíllam vitam degéntibus, glorificáre Deum Patrem omnipoténtem.

S. Let us pray.
℣. Let us kneel down.
℟. Arise.

S. Orémus.
℣. Flectámus genua.
℟. Leváte.

Almighty and everlasting God, Who in Christ hast revealed Thy glory to all nations: guard the works of Thy mercy; that Thy Church, spread over the whole world, may with steadfast faith persevere

Omnípotens sempitérne Deus, qui glóriam tuam ómnibus in Christo géntibus revelásti: custódi ópera misericórdiæ tuæ; ut Ecclésia tua, toto orbe diffúsa, stábili fide in confessióne

tui nóminis persevéret. Per eúmdem Dóminum. ℞. Amen.

in the confession of Thy Name. Through the same Lord. ℞. Amen.

FOR THE POPE

ORÉMUS et pro beatíssimo Papa N. ut Deus et Dóminus noster, qui elégit eum in órdine episcopátus, salvum atque incólumem custódiat Ecclésiæ suæ sanctæ, ad regéndum pópulum sanctum Dei.

LET US PRAY for our most holy Father N., that our Lord and God, Who chose him to the order of the Episcopate, may keep him in health and safety for His holy Church to govern the holy people of God.

S. *Orémus.*
℣. *Flectámus genua.*
℞. *Leváte.*

S. Let us pray.
℣. Let us kneel down.
℞. Arise.

Omnípotens sempitérne Deus, cujus judício univérsa fundántur: réspice propítius ad preces nostras, et eléctum nobis Antístitem tua pietáte consérva; ut christiána plebs, quæ te gubernátur auctóre, sub tanto Pontífice, credulitátis suæ méritis augeátur. Per Dóminum nostrum. ℞. Amen.

Almighty and everlasting God, by Whose judgment all things are established, mercifully regard our prayers, and in Thy goodness preserve the Bishop chosen for us: that the Christian people who are ruled by Thine authority, may under so great a Pontiff, be increased in the merits of faith. Through our Lord. ℞. Amen.

FOR ALL ORDERS AND DEGREES OF THE FAITHFUL

ORÉMUS et pro ómnibus Epíscopis, Presbýteris, Diacónibus, Subdiacónibus, Acólythis, Exorcístis, Lectóribus, Ostiáriis, Confessóribus, Virgínibus, Víduis: et pro omni pópulo sancto Dei.

LET US PRAY also for all Bishops, Priests, Deacons, Subdeacons, Acolytes, Exorcists, Readers, Porters, Confessors, Virgins, Widows, and for all the holy people of God.

S. *Orémus.*
℣. *Flectámus genua.*
℞. *Leváte.*

S. Let us pray.
℣. Let us kneel down.
℞. Arise.

Almighty and everlasting God, by Whose Spirit the whole body of the Church is sanctified and ruled, hear our humble pleading for all the orders thereof, that by the gift of Thy grace in all their several degrees may faithfully serve Thee. Through our Lord. ℟. Amen.

Omnípotens sempitérne Deus, cujus Spíritu totum corpus Ecclésiæ sanctificátur, et régitur: exáudi nos pro univérsis ordínibus supplicántes; ut grátiæ tuæ múnere, ab ómnibus tibi grádibus fidéliter serviátur. Per Dóminum nostrum. ℟. Amen.

FOR THE RULERS OF STATES

LET US PRAY for all rulers of States, their assistants and authorities, that Our Lord and God may, for our perpetual peace, direct their hearts and minds according to His Will.

ORÉMUS et pro ómnibus res públicas moderántibus, eorúmque ministériis et potestátibus: ut Deus et Dóminus noster mentes et corda eórum secúndum voluntátem suam dírigat ad nostram perpétuam pacem.

S. Let us pray.
℣. Let us kneel down.
℟. Arise.

S. *Orémus.*
℣. *Flectámus genua.*
℟. *Leváte.*

Almighty and everlasting God, in Your hands are the powers and rights of all peoples; look down graciously upon those in authority over us that, by the protection of Your right hand, soundness of religion and safety of the State may ever abide. Through our Lord. ℟. Amen.

Omnípotens sempitérne Deus, in cujus manu sunt ómnium potestátes et ómnium jura populórum: réspice benígnus ad eos, qui nos in potestáte regunt; ut ubíque terrárum, déxtera tua protegénte, et religiónis intégritas, et pátriæ secúritas indesinénter consístat. Per Dóminum nostrum. ℟. Amen.

FOR THE CATECHUMENS

LET US PRAY also for our Catechumens: that our Lord and God would open the ears of their hearts, and the gate of mercy; that having received by the font of regeneration

ORÉMUS et pro catechúmenis nostris: ut Deus et Dóminus noster adapériat aures præcordiórum ipsórum, januámque misericórdiæ; ut per lavácrum regeratiónis accépta remissióne ómnium

peccatórum, et ipsi inveniántur in Christo Jesu Dómino nostro.

the remission of all their sins, they also may be found in Christ Jesus our Lord.

S. *Orémus.*

℣. *Flectámus genua.*

℞. *Leváte.*

S. Let us pray.

℣. Let us kneel down.

℞. Arise.

Omnípotens sempitérne Deus, qui Ecclésiam tuam nova semper prole fœcúndas: auge fidem et intelléctum catechúmenis nostris; ut renáti fonte baptísmatis, adoptiónis tuæ fíliis aggregéntur. Per Dóminum nostrum. ℞. *Amen.*

Almighty and everlasting God, Who dost ever make Thy Church fruitful with new offspring: increase the faith and understanding of our Catechumens; that, being born again in the font of Baptism, they may be associated with the children of Thine adoption. Through our Lord. ℞. Amen.

FOR THE NEEDS OF THE FAITHFUL

ORÉMUS, *dilectíssimi nobis, Deum Patrem omnipoténtem, ut cunctis mundum purget erróribus: morbos áuferat: famem depéllat: apériat cárceres: víncula dissólvat: peregrinántibus réditum: infirmántibus sanitátem: navigántibus portum salútis indúlgeat.*

LET US PRAY, dearly beloved, to God the Father almighty, that He would cleanse the world of all errors: take away diseases, drive away famine, open prisons, break chains, grant a sure return to travelers, health to the sick, and a safe haven to those at sea.

S. *Orémus.*

℣. *Flectámus genua.*

℞. *Leváte.*

S. Let us pray.

℣. Let us kneel down.

℞. Arise.

Omnípotens sempitérne Deus, mæstórum consolátio, laborántium fortitúdo: pervéniant ad te preces de quacúmque tribulatióne clamántium; ut omnes sibi in necessitátibus suis misericórdiam tuam

Almighty and everlasting God, the comfort of the sorrowful, and the strength of those that labor: may the prayers of those that call upon Thee in any trouble reach Thee; that all may rejoice that in their necessities Thy mercy has helped them. Through our Lord. ℟. Amen.

gáudeant affuísse. Per Dóminum nostrum. ℟. Amen.

FOR THE UNITY OF THE CHURCH

LET US PRAY also for heretics and schismatics: that our Lord God would be pleased to rescue them from all their errors; and recall them to our holy mother the Catholic and Apostolic Church.

ORÉMUS et pro hæréticis, et schismáticis: ut Deus et Dóminus noster éruat eos ab erróribus univérsis; et ad sanctam matrem Ecclésiam Cathólicam, atque Apostólicam revocáre dignétur.

S. Let us pray.
℣. Let us kneel down.
℟. Arise.

S. *Orémus.*
℣. *Flectámus genua.*
℟. *Leváte.*

Almighty and everlasting God, Who savest all, and wouldst that no one should perish: look on the souls that are led astray by the deceit of the devil: that having set aside all heretical evil, the hearts of those that err may repent, and return to the unity of Thy truth. Through our Lord. ℟. Amen.

Omnípotens sempitérne Deus, qui salvas omnes, et néminem vis períre: réspice ad ánimas diabólica fraude decéptas; ut, omni hærética pravitáte depósita, errántium corda resipíscant, et ad veritátis tuæ rédeant unitátem. Per Dóminum nostrum. ℟. Amen.

FOR THE CONVERSION OF THE JEWS

LET US PRAY for the Jews: may our God and Lord enlighten their hearts, so that they may acknowledge Jesus Christ Savior of all men.

ORÉMUS et pro Judaéis: ut Deus et Dóminus noster illúminet corda eórum, ut agnóscant Jesum Christum salvatórem ómnium hóminum.

S. Let us pray.
℣. Let us kneel down.
℟. Arise.

S. *Orémus.*
℣. *Flectámus genua.*
℟. *Leváte.*

Almighty and Everlasting God, Who desirest that all men be saved and come to the knowledge of the truth;

Omnípotens sempitérne Deus, qui vis ut omnes hómines salvi fiant et ad agnitiónem veritátis véniant, concéde

*propítius, ut plenitúdine géntium in
Ecclésiam Tuam intránte omnis Israël
salvus fiat. Per Christum Dóminum
nostrum. ℞. Amen.*

mercifully grant that, as the fullness of
the Gentiles enters into Thy Church,
all Israel may be saved. Through Christ
our Lord. ℞. Amen.

FOR THE CONVERSION OF PAGANS

*ORÉMUS et pro pagánis: ut Deus
omnípotens áuferat iniquitátem
a córdibus eórum; ut relíctis idólis
suis, convertántur ad Deum vivum et
verum, et únicum Fílium ejus Jesum
Christum Deum et Dóminum nostrum.*

LET US PRAY also for the pagans: that
almighty God would remove iniquity
from their hearts: that, putting aside
their idols, they may be converted to
the true and living God, and His only
Son, Jesus Christ our God and Lord.

S. *Orémus.*
℣. *Flectámus genua.*
℞. *Leváte.*

S. Let us pray.
℣. Let us kneel down.
℞. Arise.

*Omnípotens sempitérne Deus, qui non
mortem peccatórum, sed vitam semper
inquíris: súscipe propítius oratiónem
nostram, et líbera eos ab idolórum
cultúra: et ággrega Ecclésiæ tuæ sanctæ,
ad laudem et glóriam nóminis tui.
Per Dóminum nostrum. ℞. Amen.*

Almighty and everlasting God, Who
ever seekest not the death but the life
of sinners: mercifully hear our prayer,
and deliver them from the worship of
idols: and join them to Thy holy Church
for the praise and glory of Thy Name.
Through our Lord. ℞. Amen.

THE ADORATION OF THE CROSS

The Celebrant intones the following antiphon three times.

*ECCE LIGNUM CRUCIS, in quo salus
mundi pepéndit. Veníte, adorémus.*

BEHOLD THE WOOD OF THE CROSS,
on which hung the Salvation of the
world. Come, let us adore.

*As the faithful come forward to venerate the Cross, the choir chants the Improperia, or
reproaches.*

℞. *PÓPULE MEUS, quid feci tibi? Aut
in quo contristávi te? Respónde mihi.*

℞. O MY PEOPLE, what have I done
to thee? Or wherein have I afflicted
thee? Answer Me.

℣. BECAUSE I LED THEE out of the land of Egypt, thou hast prepared a Cross for thy Savior.

℣. *QUIA EDÚXI TE de terra Ægýpti: parásti Crucem Salvatóri tuo.*

O holy God!
O holy God!
O Holy strong One!
O Holy strong One!
O Holy immortal One, have mercy upon us.
O Holy immortal One, have mercy upon us.

Ágios O Theós!
Sanctus Deus!
Ágios Íschyros!
Sanctus Fortis!
Ágios Athánatos, eléison imas.

Sanctus Immortális, miserére nobis.

℣. BECAUSE I LED thee out through the desert forty years: and fed thee with manna, and brought thee into a land exceeding good, thou hast prepared a Cross for thy Savior.

QUIA EDÚXI te per desértum quadragínta annis, et manna cibávi te, et introdúxi te in terram satis bonam: parásti Crucem Salvatóri tuo.

O holy God!
O holy God!
O Holy strong One!
O Holy strong One!
O Holy immortal One, have mercy upon us.
O Holy immortal One, have mercy upon us.

Ágios O Theós!
Sanctus Deus!
Ágios Íschyros!
Sanctus Fortis!
Ágios Athánatos, eléison imas.

Sanctus Immortális, miserére nobis.

℣. WHAT MORE OUGHT I to have done for thee, that I have not done? I planted thee, indeed, My most beautiful vineyard: and thou hast become exceeding bitter to Me: for in My thirst thou gavest Me vinegar to drink: and with a lance thou hast pierced the side of thy Savior.

QUID ULTRA DÉBUI fácere tibi, et non feci? Ego quidem plantávi te víneam meam speciosíssimam: et tu facta es mihi nimis amára: acéto namque sitim meam potásti, et láncea perforásti latus Salvatóri tuo.

Ágios O Theós!
Sanctus Deus!
Ágios Íschyros!
Sanctus Fortis!
Ágios Athánatos, eléison imas.

Sanctus Immortális, miserére nobis.

O holy God!
O holy God!
O Holy strong One!
O Holy strong One!
O Holy immortal One, have mercy upon us.
O Holy immortal One, have mercy upon us.

℣. *EGO PROPTER TE flagellávi Ægýptum cum primogénitis suis: et tu me flagellátum tradidísti.* ℟. *Pópule meus...*

℣. FOR THY SAKE I scourged Egypt with its first-born: and thou hast scourged Me and delivered Me up. ℟. O My people, what have I done...

℣. *Ego edúxi te de Ægýpto, demérso Pharaóne in Mare rubrum: et tu me tradidísti princípibus sacerdótum.* ℟. *Pópule meus...*

℣. I led thee out of Egypt having drowned Pharaoh in the Red Sea: and thou hast delivered Me to the chief priests. ℟. O My people, what have I done...

℣. *Ego ante te apérui mare: et tu aperuísti láncea latus meum.* ℟. *Pópule meus...*

℣. I opened the sea before thee: and thou with a spear hast opened My side. ℟. O My people, what have I done...

℣. *Ego ante te prævívi in colúmna nubis: et tu me duxísti ad prætórium Piláti.* ℟. *Pópule meus...*

℣. I went before thee in a pillar of cloud: and thou hast led Me to the judgment hall of Pilate. ℟. O My people, what have I done...

℣. *Ego te pavi manna per desértum: et tu me cecidísti álapis et flagéllis.* ℟. *Pópule meus...*

℣. I fed thee with manna in the desert; and thou hast beaten Me with blows and scourges. ℟. O My people, what have I done...

℣. *Ego te potávi aqua salútis de petra: et tu me potásti felle et acéto.* ℟. *Pópule meus...*

℣. I gave thee the water of salvation from the rock to drink: and thou hast given Me gall and vinegar. ℟. O My people, what have I done...

℣. For thy sake I struck the kings of the Chanaanites: and thou hast struck My head with a reed. ℞. O My people, what have I done...

℣. *Ego propter te Chananæórum reges percússi: et tu percussísti arúndine caput meum.* ℞. *Pópule meus...*

℣. I gave thee a royal sceptre: and thou hast given to My head a crown of thorns. ℞. O My people, what have I done...

℣. *Ego dedi tibi sceptrum regále, et tu dedísti cápiti meo spíneam corónam.* ℞. *Pópule meus...*

℣. I exalted thee with great strength: and thou hast hanged Me on the gibbet of the Cross. ℞. O My people, what have I done...

℣. *Ego te exaltávi magna virtúte: et tu me suspendísti in patíbulo Crucis.* ℞. *Pópule meus...*

2ND ANTIPHON Psalm 66: 2

WE ADORE Thy Cross, O Lord: and we praise and glorify Thy holy Resurrection: for behold by the wood of the Cross joy has come into the whole world. May God have mercy on us, and bless us: may He cause the light of His countenance to shine upon us, and have mercy on us. We adore Thy Cross, O Lord.

CRUCEM TUAM adorámus, Dómine: et sanctam resurrectiónem tuam laudámus, et glorificámus: ecce enim propter lignum venit gáudium in univérso mundo. Deus misereátur nostri, et benedícat nobis: illúminet vultum suum super nos, et misereátur nostri. Crucem tuam adorámus, Dómine.

PANGE LINGUA GLORIOSI with CRUX FIDELIS

SING, MY TONGUE, the glorious battle!
With completed victory rife!
And above the Cross' trophy
Tell the triumph of the strife:
How the world's Redeemer conquer'd
By the offering of His life.
℞. Faithful Cross! Above all other,
One and only noble Tree!
None in foliage, none in blossom,
None in fruit thy peer may be.

℣. *PANGE, LINGUA, gloriosi, lauream certaminis, et super Crucis trophaeo die triumphum nobilem: Qualiter Redemptor orbis immolatus vicerit.* ℞. *Crux fidelis, inter omnes, arbor una nobilis; Nulla silva talem profert, fronde, flore, germine.*

℣. *De parentis protoplasti, fraude Factor condolens, Quando pomi noxialis in necem morsu ruit: Ipse lignum tunc notavit, damna ligni ut solveret.* ℟. *Dulce lignum, dulces clavos, dulce pondus sustinet.*

℣. God, his Maker, sorely grieving,
That the first-made Adam fell,
When he ate the fruit of sorrow,
Whose reward was death and hell,
Noted then this Wood the ruin,
Of the ancient wood to quell.
℟. Sweetest wood and sweetest iron,
Sweetest weight is hung on thee.

℣. *Hoc opus nostrae salutis ordo deposcerat: Multiformis proditoris ars ut artem falleret, Et medelam ferret inde, hostis unde laeserat.* ℟. *Crux fidelis...*

℣. For this work of our salvation
Needs must have its order so,
And the manifold deceiver's
Art by art would overthrow,
And from thence would bring the
    healing,
Whence the insult of the foe.
℟. Faithful Cross...

℣. Wherefore when the appointed fullness
Of the holy time was come,
He was sent who maketh all things
From th' eternal Father's home,
And proceeded, God Incarnate,
Offspring of the Virgin's womb.
℟. Sweetest wood...

℣. *Quando venit ergo sacri plenitudo temporis, Missus est ab arce Patris, Natus, orbis Conditor, Atque ventre virginali carne amictus prodiit.*
℟. *Dulce lignum...*

℣. Weeps the Infant in the manger
That in Bethlehem's stable stands:
And His Limbs the Virgin Mother
Doth compose in swaddling bands,
Meetly thus in linen folding
Of her God the feet and hands.
℟. Faithful Cross...

℣. *Vagit infans inter arcta, conditus praesepia, Membra pannis involuta, Virgo Mater alligat, Et Dei manus pedesque stricta cingit fascia.*
℟. *Crux fidelis...*

℣. His appointed time fulfilled,
Born for this, He meets His Passion,
For that this He freely willed:
On the Cross the Lamb is lifted,
Where His life-blood shall be spilled.
℟. Sweetest wood...

℣. *Lustra sex qui iam peregit, tempus implens corporis, Sponte libera Redemptor, passioni deditus, Agnus in Crucis levatur immolandus stipite.*
℟. *Dulce lignum...*

℣. He endured the nails, the spitting,
Vinegar, and spear, and reed;
From that holy Body broken
Blood and water forth proceed:
Earth, and stars, and sky, and ocean,
By that flood from stain are freed.
℟. Faithful Cross...

℣. *Felle potus ecce languet; spina, clavi, lancea, Mite corpus perforarunt, unda manat et cruor; Terra, pontus, astra, mundus, quo lavantur flumine!* ℟. *Crux fidelis...*

℣. Bend thy boughs, O Tree of glory!
Thy relaxing sinews bend;
For awhile the ancient rigor,
That thy birth bestowed, suspend:
And the King of heavenly beauty

℣. *Flecte ramos, arbor alta, tensa laxa viscera, Et rigor lentescat ille, quem dedit nativitas, Et superni membra Regis tende miti stipite.*
℟. *Dulce lignum...*

On thy bosom gently tend!
℟. Sweetest wood...

℣. *Sola digna tu fuisti, ferre mundi victimam, Atque portum praeparare area mundo naufrago, Quam sacer cruor perunxit, fusus Agni corpore.*
℟. *Crux fidelis...*

℣. Thou alone wast counted worthy
This world's ransom to uphold;
For a shipwrecked race preparing
Harbor, like the Ark of old;
With the sacred Blood anointed
From the smitten Lamb that rolled.
℟. Faithful Cross...

℣. *Sempiterna sit beatae Trinitati gloria; Æqua Patri Filioque, par decus Paraclito; Unius Trinique nomen laudet universitas. Amen.*
℟. *Dulce lignum...*

℣. To the Trinity be glory
Everlasting, as is meet:
Equal to the Father, equal
To the Son, and Paraclete:
Trinal Unity, Whose praises
All created things repeat. Amen.
℟. Sweetest wood...

THE COMMUNION

COMMUNION ANTIPHONS

ADORÁMUS TE, Christe, et benedícimus tibi, quia per Crucem tuam redemísti mundum.

WE ADORE THEE, O Christ, and we bless Thee, because by Thy Cross Thou hast redeemed the world.

PER LIGNUM servi facti sumus, et per sanctam Crucem liberáti sumus: fructus árboris sedúxit nos, Fílius Dei redémit nos.

THROUGH A TREE we were enslaved, and through a holy Cross have we been set free: the fruit of a tree led us astray, the Son of God bought us back.

SALVÁTOR MUNDI, salva nos: qui per Crucem et Sánguinem tuum redemísti nos, auxiliáre nobis, te deprecámur, Deus noster.

SAVIOR OF THE WORLD, do Thou save us, do Thou, Who through Thy Cross and Blood didst redeem us, do Thou help us, our God, we beseech Thee.

The Celebrant and the faithful pray the Pater Noster *aloud. See page 23.*

POSTCOMMUNION COLLECTS

UPON Thy people who with devout hearts have recalled the Passion and Death of Thy Son, we beseech Thee, O Lord, may plentiful blessings descend: may gentleness be used with us, and consolation given us, may our faith increase in holiness, our redemption for ever made firm. Through the same Christ our Lord. ℟. Amen.

SUPER populum tuum, quaesumus, Domine, qui passionem et mortem Filii tui devota mente recoluit, benedictio copiosa descendat, indulgentia veniat, consolatio tribuatur, fides sancta succrescat, redemptio sempiterna firmetur. Per eundem Christum Dominum nostrum. ℟. Amen.

ALMIGHTY and merciful God, Who hast restored us by the Passion and Death of Thy Christ: preserve within us the work of Thy mercy; that by our entering into this mystery we may ever live devoutly. Through the same Christ our Lord. ℟. Amen.

OMNIPOTENS et misericors Deus, qui Christi tui beata passione et morte nos reparasti: conserva in nobis operam misericordiae tuae, ut huius mysterii participatione, perpetua devotione vivamus. Per eundem Christum Dominum nostrum. ℟. Amen.

BE MINDFUL of Thy mercies, O Lord, and hallow with eternal protection us Thy servants, from whom Christ Thy Son established through His Blood this mystery of the Pasch. Through the same Christ our Lord. ℟. Amen.

REMINISCERE miserationum tuarum, Domine, et famulos tuos aeterna protectione sanctifica, pro quibus Christus, Filius tuus, per suum cruorem, instituit paschale mysterium. Per eundem Christum Dominum nostrum. ℟. Amen.

✠ ✠ ✠

EASTER VIGIL

White   *First Class*

The sun has set on Holy Saturday. The church remains shrouded in darkness until the Gloria, that we may see the One True Light that is Christ. The liturgy begins outside, at the entrance to the church, with the blessing of new fire.

THE BLESSING OF THE NEW FIRE

℣. *Dóminus vobíscum.*

℟. *Et cum spíritu tuo.*

℣. *Orémus.*

℣. The Lord be with you.

℟. And with thy spirit.

℣. Let us pray.

DEUS, *qui per Filíum tuum, angulárem scílicet lápidem, claritátis tuæ ignem fidélibus contulísti: prodúctum e sílice, nostris profutúrum úsibus, novum hanc ignem sanctí ✠ fica: et concéde nobis, ita per hæc festa paschália cæléstibus desidériis inflammári; ut ad perpétuæ claritátis, puris méntibus, valeámus festa pertíngere. Per eúmdem Christum Dóminum nostrum. ℟. Amen.*

O GOD, Who hast bestowed on the faithful the fire of Thy brightness through Thy Son, Who is the Cornerstone, hallow ✠ this new fire produced from a flint that it may be profitable to us: and grant that during this Paschal festival we may be so inflamed with heavenly desires, that with pure minds we may come to the solemnity of perpetual light. Through the same Christ our Lord. ℟. Amen.

The Celebrant sprinkles the new fire with holy water and incenses it.

THE BLESSING OF THE PASCHAL CANDLE

The Celebrant draws the first and last letters of the Greek alphabet on the Paschal Candle, because Christ is the Beginning and the End of all things.

CHRISTUS *heri et hodie*

Principium et Finis

Alpha et Omega

Ipsius sunt tempora et saecula

Ipsi gloria et imperium per universa

seternitatis saecula. Amen.

CHRIST yesterday and today

Beginning and End

Alpha and Omega

His are the times and the ages

To Him be glory and dominion through all ages of eternity. Amen.

He fixes five grains of incense in the candle, representing the five wounds which remained in our Lord's Body after His Resurrection. The Paschal Candle is then lit from the new fire and blessed.

THROUGH HIS WOUNDS holy and glorious guard and preserve us, Christ the Lord. Amen.

PER SUA SANCTA VULNERA et gloriosa custodiat et conservet nos Christus Dominus. Amen.

LIGHT OF CHRIST, in glory rising, dispel dark night from heart and mind.

LUMEN CHRISTI gloriose resurgentis, Dissipet tenebras cordis et mentis.

℣. The Lord be with you.
℟. And with thy spirit.
℣. Let us pray.

℣. Dóminus vobíscum.
℟. Et cum spíritu tuo.
℣. Orémus.

MAY the abundant outpouring of Thy ✠ blessing, we beseech Thee, almighty God, descend upon this lighted candle; and do Thou, O invisible Regenerator, lighten this nocturnal brightness, that not only the sacrifice that is offered this night may shine by the secret mixture of Thy light: but also into whatever place anything of this mysterious sanctification shall be brought, there the power of Thy Majesty may be present and all the malicious artifices of Satan may be defeated. Through Christ our Lord. ℟. Amen.

VENIAT, quaesumus, omnipotens Deus, super hunc incensum cereum larga tuae bene ✠ dictionis infusio: et hunc nocturnum splendorem, invisibilis regenerator, intende; ut non solum sacrificium, quod hac nocte litatum est, arcana luminis tui admixtione refulgeat; sed in quocumque loco ex huius sanctificationis mysterio aliquid fuerit deportatum, expulsa diabolicae fraudis nequitia, virtus tuae maiestatis assistat. Per Christum Dominum nostrum. ℟. Amen.

THE PROCESSION WITH THE PASCHAL CANDLE

As the Easter Candle approaches the Altar, the deacon sings three times, and the sacred ministers respond.

℣. THE LIGHT OF CHRIST.
℟. Thanks be to God.

℣. LUMEN CHRISTI.
℟. Deo Grátias.

THE PASCHAL PROCLAMATION

Like a fire that spreads to the ends of the earth, light from the Paschal Candle is used to light candles held by the congregation and the Exsúltet *is sung.*

THE EXSÚLTET

EXSÚLTET *iam Angélica turba coelórum: exsúltent divína mystéria: et pro tanti Regis victória tuba ínsonet salutáris.*

Gáudeat et tellus tantis irradiáta fulgóribus: et ætérni Regis splendóre illustráta, totíus orbis se séntiat amisísse calíginem.

Lætétur et mater Ecclésia, tanti lúminis adornáta fulgóribus: et magnis populórum vócibus hæc aula resúltet.

Quaprópter astántes vos, fratres caríssimi, ad tam miram huius sancti lúminis claritátem, una mecum, quæso, Dei omnipoténtis misericórdiam invocáte. Ut, qui me non meis méritis intra Levitárum númerum dignatus est aggregáre: lúminis sui claritátem infúndens, Cérei huius laudem implére perfíciat.

Per Dominum nostrum Jesum Christum, Fílium suum: qui cum eo vivit et regnat in unitáte Spíritus Sancti Deus: Per omnia sǽcula sæculórum. R̞. Amen.

LET THE ANGELIC choirs of Heaven now rejoice; let the divine mysteries rejoice; and let the trumpet of salvation sound forth the victory of so great a King.

Let the earth also rejoice, made radiant by such splendor; and, enlightened with the brightness of the eternal King, let it know that the darkness of the whole world is scattered.

Let our Mother the Church also rejoice, adorned with the brightness of so great a light; and let this temple resound with the loud acclamations of the people.

Wherefore I beseech you, most beloved brethren, who are here present in the wondrous brightness of this holy light, to invoke with me the mercy of almighty God. That He who has vouchsafed to admit me among the Levites, without any merits of mine, would pour forth the brightness of His light upon me, and enable me to perfect the praise of this wax candle.

Through our Lord Jesus Christ His Son, Who with Him and the Holy Ghost liveth and reigneth, one God, for ever and ever. R̞. Amen.

℣. The Lord be with you.

℟. And with thy spirit.

℣. Lift up your hearts.

℟. We have lifted them up unto the Lord.

℣. Let us give thanks unto the Lord our God.

℟. It is meet and just.

IT IS TRULY MEET AND RIGHT to proclaim with all our heart and all the affection of our mind, and with the ministry of our voices, the invisible God, the Father almighty, and His only-begotten Son, our Lord Jesus Christ, Who repaid for us to His eternal Father the debt of Adam, and by the merciful shedding of His Blood, cancelled the guilt incurred by original sin.

FOR THIS is the Paschal Festival; in which that true Lamb is slain, with Whose Blood the doorposts of the faithful are consecrated.

This is the night in which Thou didst formerly cause our forefathers, the children of Israel, when brought out of Egypt, to pass through the Red Sea with dry foot.

This, therefore, is the night which dissipated the darkness of sinners by the light of the pillar.

This is the night which at this time throughout the world restores to grace and unites in sanctity those that believe

℣. *Dóminus vobíscum.*

℟. *Et cum Spíritu tuo.*

℣. *Sursum corda.*

℟. *Habémus ad Dóminum.*

℣. *Grátias agámus Dómino Deo nostro.*

℟. *Dignum et iustum est.*

VERE DIGNUM ET IUSTUM EST, invísibilem Deum Patrem omnipoténtem Filiúmque eius unigénitum, Dominum nostrum Jesum Christum, toto cordis ac mentis afféctu et vocis ministério personáre. Qui pro nobis ætérno Patri Adæ débitum solvit: et véteris piáculi cautiónem pio cruóre detérsit.

HÆC SUNT ENIM festa paschália, in quibus verus ille Agnus occíditur, cuius sánguine postes fidelium consecrántur.

Hæc nox est, in qua primum patres nostros, fílios Israël edúctos de Ægýpto, Mare Rubrum sicco vestígio transire fecísti.

Hæc ígitur nox est, quæ peccatórum ténebras colúmnæ illuminatióne purgávit.

Hæc nox est, quæ hódie per univérsum mundum in Christo credéntes, a vítiis sǽculi et calígine peccatórum

segregátos, reddit grátiæ, sóciat sanctitáti.

Hæc nox est, in qua, destrúctis vínculis mortis, Christus ab ínferis victor ascéndit. Nihil enim nobis nasci prófuit, nisi rédimi profuísset.

O mira circa nos tuæ pietátis dignátio!

O inæstimábilis diléctio caritátis: ut servum redimeres, Fílium tradidísti!

O certe necessárium Adæ peccátum, quod Christi morte delétum est! O felix culpa, quæ talem ac tantum méruit habére Redemptórem! O vere beáta nox, quæ sola méruit scire tempus et horam, in qua Christus ab ínferis resurréxit! Hæc nox est, de qua scriptum est: Et nox sicut dies illuminábitur: Et nox illuminátio mea in deliciis meis.

Huius ígitur sanctificátio noctis fugat scélera, culpas lavat: et reddit innocéntiam lapsis et mæstis lætítiam. Fugat ódia, concórdiam parat et curvat impéria.

In huius ígitur noctis grátia, súscipe, sancte Pater, incénsi huius sacrifícium vespertínum: quod tibi in hac Cérei oblatióne solémni, per ministrórum

in Christ, and are separated from the vices of the world and the darkness of sinners.

This is the night in which, destroying the chains of death, Christ arose victorious from the grave. For it would have profited us nothing to have been born, unless redemption had also been bestowed upon us.

O wondrous condescension of Thy mercy towards us!

O inestimable affection of love: that Thou mightest redeem a slave, Thou didst deliver up Thy Son!

O truly needful sin of Adam, which was blotted out by the death of Christ!

O happy fault, that merited to possess such and so great a Redeemer!

O truly blessed night, which alone deserved to know the time and hour when Christ rose again from hell!

This is the night of which it is written: And the night shall be as clear as the day; and the night is my light in my delights.

Therefore the hallowing of this night puts to flight all wickedness, cleanses sins, and restores innocence to the fallen, and gladness to the sorrowful. It drives forth hatreds, it prepares concord, and brings down haughtiness.

Wherefore, in this sacred night, receive, O holy Father, the evening sacrifice of this incense, which holy Church renders to Thee by the hands of Thy ministers in the solemn offering of this wax candle, made out of the work of bees.

Now also we know the praises of this pillar, which the shining fire enkindles to the honor of God. Which fire, although divided into parts, suffers no loss from its light being borrowed. For it is nourished by the melting wax, which the mother bee produced for the substance of this precious light.

O truly blessed night, which plundered the Egyptians and enriched the Hebrews! A night in which heavenly things are united to those of earth, and things divine to those which are of man.

We beseech Thee, therefore, O Lord, that this wax candle hallowed in honor of Thy Name, may continue to burn to dissipate the darkness of this night. And being accepted as a sweet savor, may be united with the heavenly lights. Let the morning star find its flame alight. That star, I mean, which knows no setting. He Who returning from hell, serenely shone forth upon mankind.

We beseech Thee therefore, O Lord, that Thou wouldst grant peaceful times during this Paschal Festival, and vouchsafe to rule, govern, and keep with Thy constant protection us Thy servants, and all the clergy, and the devout people, together with our most holy Father, Pope N., and our Bishop N.

manus de opéribus apum, sacrosáncta reddit Ecclésia.

Sed iam colúmnæ huius præcónia nóvimus, quam in honórem Dei rútilans ignis accéndit. Qui licet sit divísus in partes, mutuáti tamen lúminis detriménta non novit. Alitur enim liquántibus ceris, quas in substántiam pretiósæ huius lámpadis apis mater edúxit.

O vere beáta nox, quæ exspoliávit Ægýptios, ditávit Hebræos! Nox, in qua terrénis cæléstia, humánis divína iungúntur.

Orámus ergo te, Dómine: ut Céreus iste in honórem tui nóminis consecrátus, ad noctis huius calíginem destruéndam, indefíciens persevéret. Et in odórem suavitátis accéptus, supérnis lumináribus misceátur. Flammas eius lúcifer matutínus invéniat. Ille, inquam, lúcifer, qui nescit occásum. Ille, qui regréssus ab ínferis, humáno géneri serénus illúxit.

Precámur ergo te, Dómine: ut nos fámulos tuos, omnémque clerum, et devotíssimum pópulum: una cum beatíssimo Papa nostro N., et Antístite nostro N., quiéte témporum concéssa, in his paschálibus gáudiis, assídua protectióne régere, gubernáre et conserváre dignéris.

Réspice étiam ad eos, qui nos in potestáte regunt, et, ineffábili pietátis et misericórdiæ tuæ múnere, dírige cogitatiónes eórum ad iustítiam et pacem, ut de terréna operositáte ad cæléstem pátriam pervéniant cum omni populo tuo.

Per eúndem Dóminum nostrum Jesum Christum, Fílium tuum: Qui tecum vivit et regnat in unitáte Spíritus Sancti Deus: per ómnia sǽcula sæculórum. ℟. Amen.

Have regard, also, for those who reign over us, and grant them Thine ineffable kindness and mercy, direct their thoughts in justice and peace, that from their earthy toil, they may come to their heavenly reward with all Thy people.

Through the same Jesus Christ Thy Son, our Lord, who with Thee lives and reigns in the unity of the Holy Ghost, God, world without end ℟. Amen.

THE PROPHECIES

1ST READING *Genesis 1: 1-31; 2: 1, 2*

IN PRINCIPIO creavit Deus cælum et terram. Terra autem erat inanis et vacua, et tenebræ erant super faciem abyssi: et Spiritus Dei ferebatur super aquas. Dixitque Deus: Fiat lux. Et facta est lux. Et vidit Deus lucem quod esset bona: et divisit lucem a tenebris.

IN THE BEGINNING God created heaven and earth. And the earth was void and empty, and darkness was upon the face of the deep: and the Spirit of God moved over the waters. And God said: Be light made. And light was made. And God saw the light, that it was good, and He divided the light from the darkness. And He called the light Day, and the darkness Night: and there was evening and morning, one day. And God said: Let there be a firmament made amidst the waters: and let it divide the waters from the waters. And God made a firmament, and divided the waters that were under the firmament from those that were above the firmament. And it was so. And God called the firmament Heaven: and the evening and morning were the second day. God also said: Let the waters that are under the heaven be gathered together into one place; and let the dry land appear. And it was so done. And God called the dry land Earth: and the gathering together of the waters He called Seas. And God saw that it was good. And He said: Let the earth bring forth the green herb, and such as may seed, and the fruit tree yielding fruit after its kind, which may have seed in itself upon the earth. And it was so done. And the earth brought forth the green herb, and such as yieldeth seed according to its kind, and the tree that beareth fruit having seed, each one according to its kind. And God saw that it was good. And the evening and morning were the third day. And God said: Let there be lights made in the firmament

Appellavitque lucem Diem, et tenebras Noctem: factumque est vespere et mane, dies unus. Dixit quoque Deus: Fiat firmamentum in medio aquarum: et dividat aquas ab aquis. Et fecit Deus firmamentum, divisitque aquas quæ erant sub firmamento, ab his quæ erant super firmentum. Et factum est ita. Vocavit Deus firmamentum Cælum: et factum est vespere et mane, dies secundus. Dixit vero Deus: Congregentur aquæ, quæ sub cælo sunt, in locum unum: et appareat arida. Et factum est ita. Et vocavit Deus aridam, Terram, congregationisque aquarum appellavit Maria. Et vidit Deus quod esset bonum. Et ait: Germinet terra herbam virentem, et facientem semen, et lignum pomiferum faciens fructum iuxta genus suum, cuius semen in semetipso sit super terram. Et factum est ita. Et protulit terra herbam virentem, et facientem semen iuxta genus suum, lignumque faciens fructum, et habens unumquodque sementem secundum speciem suam. Et vidit Deus quod esset bonum. Et factum est vespere et mane, dies tertius. Dixit autem Deus: Fiant luminaria in firmamento cæli, et dividant diem ac noctem, et sint in signa et tempora, et dies et annos: ut luminent terram. Et factum est ita. Fecitque Deus duo luminaria magna: luminare maius, ut præesset diei, et luminare minus, ut præesset nocti: et stellas. Et posuit eas in firmamento cæli, ut lucerent super terram, et præessent diei ac nocti, et dividerent lucem ac tenebras. Et vidit Deus quod esset bonum. Et factum est vespere et mane, dies quartus. Dixit etiam Deus: Producant aquæ reptile animæ viventis, et volatile super terram sub firmamento cæli. Creavitque Deus cete grandia, et omnem animam viventem atque motabilem, quam produxerant aquæ in species suas, et omne volatile secundum genus suum. Et vidit Deus quod esset bonum. Benedixitque eis, dicens: Crescite, et multiplicamini, et replete aquas maris: avesque multiplicentur super terram. Et factum est vespere et mane, dies quintus. Dixit quoque Deus: Producat terra animam viventem in genere suo: iumenta, et reptilia, et bestias terræ secundum species suas. Factumque est ita. Et fecit Deus quod esset bonum, et ait: Faciamus hominem ad imaginem et similitudinem nostram: et præsit piscibus maris, et volatilibus cæli, et bestiis, universæque terræ, omnique reptili quod movetur in terra. Et creavit Deus hominem ad imaginem suam: ad imaginem Dei creavit illum, masculum et feminam creavit eos. Benedixitque illis Deus, et ait: Crescite et multiplicamini, et replete terram, et

of heaven to divide the day and the night, and let them be for signs, and for seasons, and for days and years: to shine in the firmament of heaven, and to give light upon the earth. And it was so done. And God made two great lights: a greater light to rule the day; and a lesser light to rule the night, and the stars. And He set them in the firmament of heaven, to shine upon the earth, and to rule the day and the night, and to divide the light and the darkness. And God saw that it was good. And the evening and morning were the fourth day. God also said: Let the waters bring forth the creeping creature having life, and the fowl that may fly over the earth under the firmament of heaven. And God created the great whales, and every living and moving creature which the waters brought forth, according to their kinds, and every winged fowl according to its kind. And God saw that it was good. And He blessed them, saying: Increase and multiply, and fill the waters of the sea: and let the birds be multiplied upon the earth. And the evening and the morning were the fifth day. And God said: Let the earth bring forth the living creature in its kind, cattle, and creeping things, and beasts of the earth according to their kinds. And it was so done. And God made the beasts of the earth according to their kinds, and cattle, and every thing that creepeth on the earth after its kind. And God saw that it was good. And He said: Let Us make man to Our own image and likeness: and let him have dominion over the fishes of the sea, and the fowls of the air, and the beasts, and the whole earth, and every creeping creature that moveth upon the earth. And God created man to His own image: to the image of God He created him, male and female He created them. And God blessed them, saying: Increase and multiply, and fill the earth, and subdue it, and rule over the fishes of the sea, and the fowls of the air, and all living creatures that move upon the earth. And God said: Behold, I have given you every herb bearing seed upon the earth, and all trees that have in themselves seed of their own kind, to be your meat: and to all the beasts of the earth, and to

subicite eam, et dominamini piscibus maris, et volatilibus cæli, et universis animantibus, quæ moventur super terram. Dixitque Deus: Ecce dedi vobis omnem herbam afferentem semen super terram, et universa ligna quæ habent in semetipsis sementum generis sui, ut sint vobis in escam: et cunctis animantibus terræ, omnique volucri cæli, et universis, quæ moventur in terra, et in quibus est anima vivens, ut habeant ad vescendum. Et factum est ita. Viditque Deus cuncta quæ fecerat: et erant valde bona. Et factum est vespere et mane, dies sextus. Igitur perfecti sunt cæli et terra, et omnis ornatus eorum. Complevitque Deus die septimo opus suum quod fecerat: et requievit die septimo ab universo opere quod patrarat.

every fowl of the air, and to all that move upon the earth, and wherein there is life, that they may have to feed upon. And it was so done. And God saw all the things that He had made, and they were very good. And the evening and morning were the sixth day. So the heavens and the earth were finished, and all the furniture of them. And on the seventh day God ended His work which He had made: and He rested on the seventh day from all His work which He had done.

℣. The Lord be with you.
℟. And with thy spirit.
℣. Let us pray.

S. *Orémus.*
℣. *Flectámus génua.*
℟. *Leváte.*

DEUS, qui mirabiliter creasti hominem, et mirabilius redemisti: da nobis, quaesumus, contra oblectamenta peccati, mentis ratione persistere, ut mereamur ad aeterna gaudia pervenire. Per Dominum nostrum. R/. Amen.

O GOD, Who hast wonderfully created man, and more wonderfully redeemed him: grant us, we beseech Thee, to stand firm with strong minds against the allurements of sin, that we may deserve to arrive at everlasting joys. Through our Lord. R/. Amen.

2ND READING *Exodus 14: 24-31; 15: 1*

IN DIEBUS ILLIS: Factum est in vigilia matutina, et ecce respiciens Dominus super castra Ægyptiorum per columnam ignis et nubis, interfecit exercitum eorum: et subvertit rotas curruum, ferebanturque in profundum. Dixerunt ergo Ægyptii: Fugiamus Israelem: Dominus enim pugnat pro eis contra nos. Et ait Dominus ad Moysen: Extende manum tuam super mare, ut revertantur aquae ad Ægyptios super currus et equites eorum. Cumque extendisset Moyses manum contra mare, reversum est primo diluculo ad priorem locum: fugientibusque Ægyptiis occurrerunt aquae, et involvit eos Dominus in mediis fluctibus. Reversaeque sunt aquae, et operuerunt currus et equites cuncti exercitus Pharaonis, qui sequentes ingressi fuerant mare: nec unus quidem superfuit ex eis. Filii autem Israel perrexerunt per medium sicci maris, et aquae eis erant quasi pro muro a dextris et a sinistris: liberavitque Dominus in die illa Israel

I N THOSE DAYS, it came to pass in the morning watch, and behold the Lord looking upon the Egyptian army through the pillar of fire and of the cloud, slew their host: and overthrew the wheels of the chariots, and they were carried into the deep. And the Egyptians said: Let us flee from Israel: for the Lord fighteth for them against us. And the Lord said to Moses: Stretch forth thy hand over the sea, that the waters may come again upon the Egyptians, upon their chariots and horsemen. And when Moses had stretched forth his hand towards the sea, it returned at the first break of day to the former place: and as the Egyptians were fleeing away the waters came upon them, and the Lord shut them up in the middle of the waves. And the waters returned, and covered the chariots and the horsemen of all the army of Pharaoh, who had come into the sea after them: neither did there so much as one of them remain. But the children of Israel marched through the midst of the sea upon dry land, and the waters were to them as a wall on the right hand and on the left: and the Lord delivered Israel on that day out of the hand of the Egyptians. And they saw the Egyptians dead upon the sea shore, and the mighty hand that the Lord had used against them: and the people feared the Lord, and they believed the Lord, and Moses His servant. Then Moses and the children of Israel sung this canticle to the Lord, and said:

de manu Ægyptiorum. Et viderunt Ægyptios mortuos super littus maris, et manum magnam, quam exercuerat Dominus contra eos: timuitque populus Dominum, et crediderunt Domino, et Moysi servo eius. Tunc cecinit Moyses, et filii Israel carmen hoc Domino, et dixerunt:

CANTICLE *Exodus 15: 1, 2*

LET US SING TO THE LORD, for He is gloriously honored: the horse and the rider He hath thrown into the sea: He has become my Helper and Protector unto salvation. He is my God, and I will honor Him: the God of my father, and I will extol Him. He is the Lord that destroys wars: the Lord is His Name.

CANTEMUS DOMINO: gloriose enim honorificatus est: equum et ascensorem proiecit in mare: adiutor et protector factus est mihi in salutem. Hic Deus meus, et honorificabo eum: Deus patris mei, et exaltabo eum. Dominus conterens bella: Dominus nomen est illi.

S. Let us pray.
℣. Let us kneel.
℟. Arise.

S. *Orémus.*
℣. *Flectámus génua.*
℟. *Leváte.*

O GOD, Whose ancient miracles we see shining also in our days, whilst by the water of regeneration Thou dost operate for the salvation of the Gentiles, that which by the power of Thy right hand Thou didst confer upon one people by delivering them from

DEUS, cuius antiqua miracula etiam nostris saeculis coruscare sentimus: dum quod uni populo, a persecutione Ægyptiaca liberando, dexterae tuae potentia contulisti, id in salutem gentium per aquam regenerationis operaris: praesta, ut in Abrahae

filios, et in Israeliticam dignitatem,
totius mundi transeat plenitude.
Per Dominum nostrum. ℟. *Amen.*

the Egyptian persecution: grant that all the nations of the world may become the children of Abraham, and partake of the dignity of the people of Israel. Through our Lord. ℟. Amen.

3RD READING *Isaiah 4: 2-6*

IN DIE ILLA erit germen Domini in magnificentia et gloria, et fructus terrae sublimis, et exsultatio his, qui salvati fuerint de Israel. Et erit: Omnis qui relictus fuerit in Sion, et residuus in Ierusalem, sanctus vocabitur, omnis qui scriptus est in vita in Ierusalem. Si abluerit Dominus sordes filiarum Sion, et sanguinem Ierusalem laverit de medio eius, in spiritu iudicii et spiritu ardoris. Et creabit Dominus super omnem locum montis Sion, et ubi invocatus est, nubem per diem, et fumum et splendorem ignis flam-mantis in nocte: super omnem enim gloriam protectio. Et tabernaculum erit in umbraculum diei ab aestu, et in securitatem, et absconsionem a turbine, et a pluvia.

IN THAT DAY the bud of the Lord shall be in magnificence and glory, and the fruit of the earth shall be high, and a great joy to them that shall have escaped of Israel. And it shall come to pass, that every one that shall be left in Sion, and that shall remain in Jerusalem, shall be called holy, every one that is written in life in Jerusalem, if the Lord shall wash away the filth of the daughters of Sion, and shall wash away the blood of Jerusalem out of the midst thereof, by the spirit of judgment and by the spirit of burning. And the Lord will create upon every place of Mount Sion, and where He is called upon, a cloud by day, and a smoke and the brightness of a flaming fire in the night: for over all the glory shall be a protection. And there shall be a tabernacle for a shade in the daytime from the heat, and for a security and covert from the whirlwind, and from rain.

CANTICLE *Isaiah 5: 1, 2, 7*

VINEA FACTA EST dilecto in cornu, in loco uberi. Et maceriam circumdedit, et circumfodit: et plantavit vineam

MY BELOVED had a vineyard on a hill in a fruitful place. And he enclosed it with a fence, and made a ditch round it, and planted it with the vine of Sorec, and built a tower in the midst thereof. And he made a winepress in it: for the vineyard of the Lord of hosts is the house of Israel.

Sorec, et aedificavit turrim in medio eius. Et torcular fodit in ea: vinea enim Domini Sabaoth, domus Israel est.

S. Let us pray.
℣. Let us kneel.
℟. Arise.

S. *Orémus.*
℣. *Flectámus génua.*
℟. *Leváte.*

O GOD, Who by the voice of the holy prophets hast declared to all the children of Thy Church that through the whole extent of Thine empire Thou art the Sower of good seed, and the Cultivator of chosen branches: grant to Thy people who are called by Thee, by the name of vines and harvest field, that they may root out all thorns and briars, and produce good fruit in abundance. Through our Lord. ℟. Amen.

DEUS, *qui in omnibus Ecclesiae tuae filiis sanctorum prophetarum voce manifestasti, in omni loco dominationis tuae, satorem te bonorum seminum, et electorum palmitum esse cultorem: tribue populis tuis, qui et vinearum apud te nomine censentur et segetum; ut, spinarum et tribulorum squalore resecato, digna efficiantur fruge fecundi. Per Dominum nostrum.* ℟. Amen.

4TH READING *Deuteronomy 31: 22-30*

IN THOSE DAYS: Moses therefore wrote the canticle, and taught it to the children of Israel. And the Lord commanded Josue the son of Nun, and said: Take courage, and be valiant: for thou shalt bring the children of Israel into the land which I have promised, and I will be with thee. Therefore after Moses wrote the words of this law in a volume, and finished it: he commanded the Levites, who carried the ark of the covenant of the Lord, saying: Take this book, and put it in

IN DIEBUS ILLIS: *Scripsit Moyses canticum, et docuit filios Israel. Praecepitque Dominus Josue filio Nun, et ait: Confortare, et esto robustus: tu enim introduces filios Israel in terram, quam pollicitus sum, et ego ero tecum. Postquam ergo scripsit Moyses verba legis huius in volumine, atque complevit: praecepit Levitis, qui portabant arcam foederis Domini, dicens: Tollite librum istum, et ponite eum in latere arcae foederis Domini Dei vestri: ut sit ibi* contra te in testimonium. Ego enim scio contentionem tuam, et cervicem tuam durissimam. Adhuc vivente me, et ingrediente vobiscum, semper contentiose egistis contra Dominum: quanto magis cum mortuus fuero? Congregate ad me omnes maiores natu per tribus vestras, atque doctores, et loquar audientibus eis sermones istos, et invocabo contra eos caelum et terram. Novi enim quod post mortem meam inique agetis, et declinabitis cito de via, quam praecepi vobis: et occurrent vobis mala in extremo tempore, quando feceritis malum in conspectu Domini, ut irritetis eum per opera manuum vestrarum. Locutus est ergo Moyses, audiente universo coetu Israel, verba carminis huius, et ad finem usque complevit:

the side of the ark of the covenant of the Lord your God: that it may be there for a testimony against thee. For I know thy obstinacy and thy most stiff neck. While I am yet living, and going in with you, you have always been rebellious against the Lord: how much more when I shall be dead? Gather unto me all the ancients of your tribes, and your doctors, and I will speak these words in their hearing, and will call heaven and earth to witness against them. For I know that after my death, you will do wickedly and will quickly turn aside from the way that I have commanded you: and evils shall come upon you in the latter times, when you shall do evil in the sight of the Lord, to provoke Him by the works of your hands. Moses therefore spoke in the hearing of the whole assembly of Israel the words of this canticle, and finished it even to the end:

CANTICLE *Deuteronomy 32: 1-4*

ATTENDE, caelum, et loquar: et audiat terra verba ex ore meo. Exspectetur sicut pluvia eloquium meum: et descendant sicut ros verba mea. Sicut imber super gramen, et sicut nix super faenum: quia nomen Domini invocabo. Date magnitudinem Deo nostro: Deus, vera opera eius, et omnes viae eius iudicia. Deus fidelis, in quo non est iniquitas: iustus

ATTEND, O Heaven, and I will speak: and let the earth hear the words that come out of my mouth. Let my speech be expected like the rain: and let my words fall like the dew. Like the shower upon the grass, and like the snow upon the dry herb, because I will invoke the Name of the Lord. Confess the greatness of our Lord: the works of God are perfect, and all His ways are justice.

God is faithful, in Whom there is no iniquity: the Lord is just and holy.

et sanctus Dominus.

S. Let us pray.
℣. Let us kneel.
℟. Arise.

S. *Orémus.*
℣. *Flectámus génua.*
℟. *Leváte.*

O GOD, the exaltation of the humble, and the strength of the righteous, Who, by Thy holy servant Moses, wast pleased so to instruct Thy people by the singing of Thy sacred canticle, that the renewal of the law should be also our guidance: show forth Thy power to all the multitude of Gentiles justified by Thee, and by mitigating Thy terror grant them joy: that, all sins being blotted out by Thy remission, the threatened vengeance may give way to salvation. Through our Lord. ℟. Amen.

DEUS, *celsitudo humilium et fortitudo rectorum, qui per sanctum Moysen puerum tuum ita erudire populum tuum sacri carminis tui decantatione voluisti, ut illa legis iteratio fieret etiam nostra directio: excita in omnem iustificatarum gentium plenitudinem potentiam tuam, et da laetitiam, mitigando terrorem, ut omnium peccatis tua remissione deletis, quod denuntiatum est in ultionem, transeat in salutem. Per Dominum nostrum.* ℟. *Amen.*

THE FIRST PART OF THE LITANIES

The congregation kneels for the Litanies.

Lord have mercy on us.
Christ have mercy on us.
Lord, have mercy.
Christ, hear us.
Christ, graciously hear us.

KÝRIE ELÉISON.
Christe eléison.
Kýrie eléison.
Christe, audi nos.
Christe, exáudi nos

God the Father of Heaven, †

Pater de célis, Deus,
miserére nobis.

God the Son, Redeemer of the world,
God the Holy Ghost,
Holy Trinity, one God,

Fili Redémptor mundi, Deus, †
Spíritus Sancte, Deus,
Sancta Trínitas, unus Deus,

† have mercy on us.

† *miserére nobis.*

Sancta María, ora pro nobis	Holy Mary, *pray for us.*
Sancta Dei Génetrix,*	Holy Mother of God,*
Sancta Virgo vírginum,	Holy Virgin of virgins,
Sancte Míchaël,	Saint Michael,
Sancte Gábriel,	Saint Gabriel,
Sancte Ráphaël,	Saint Raphael,
Omnes sancti Angeli et Archángeli,	All ye holy Angels and Archangels,
Omnes sancti beatórum Spiríttuum órdines,	All ye holy orders of blessed Spirits,
Sancte Ioánnes Baptísta, ora pro nobis.	Saint John the Baptist,
Sancte Ioseph,	Saint Joseph,
Omnes sancte Patriárchæ et Prophétæ,	All ye holy Patriarchs and Prophets,
Sancte Petre,	Saint Peter,
Sancte Paule,	Saint Paul,
Sancte Andréa,	Saint Andrew,
Sancte Ioánnes,	Saint John,
Omnes sancti Apóstoli et Evangelístæ,	All ye holy Apostles and Evangelists,
Omnes sancti Discípuli Dómini,	All ye holy Disciples of the Lord,
Sancte Stéphane, ora pro nobis.	Saint Stephen,
Sancte Laurénti,	Saint Lawrence,
Sancte Vincénti,	Saint Vincent,
Omnes sancti Mártyres,	All ye holy Martyrs,
Sancte Silvéster, ora pro nobis.	Saint Sylvester,
Sancte Gregóri,	Saint Gregory,
Sancte Augustíne,	Saint Augustine,
Omnes sancti Pontífices et Confessóres,	All ye holy Bishops and Confessors,
Omnes sancti Doctóres,	All ye holy Doctors,
Sancte Antóni, ora pro nobis.	Saint Anthony,
Sancte Benedícte,	Saint Benedict,
Sancte Domínice,	Saint Dominic,
Sancte Francísce,	Saint Francis,
Omnes sancti Sacerdótes et Levítæ,	All ye holy Priests and Levites,
Omnes sancti Mónachi et Eremítæ,	All ye holy Monks and Hermits,

* pray for us.   * ora(te) pro nobis.

Saint Mary Magdalene,	*Sancta María Magdaléna,*
Saint Agnes,	*Sancta Agnes,*
Saint Cecilia,	*Sancta Cæcília,*
Saint Agatha,	*Sancta Agatha,*
Saint Anastasia,	*Sancta Anastásia,*
All ye holy Virgins and Widows,	*Omnes sanctæ Vírgines et Víduæ,*
All ye holy men and women,	*Omnes Sancti et Sanctæ Dei,*
intercede for us.	*intercédite pro nobis.*

THE BLESSING OF BAPTISMAL WATER

The Paschal Candle is dipped into new water as a sign that the Sacrament of Baptism derives its power from Christ.

℣. The Lord be with you.

℟. And with thy spirit.

℣. Let us pray.

℣. *Dóminus vobíscum.*

℟. *Et cum spíritu tuo.*

℣. *Orémus.*

O ALMIGHTY and everlasting God, be present at these Mysteries, be present at these Sacraments of Thy great loving kindness: and send forth the spirit of adoption to regenerate a new people whom the font of baptism brings forth; that what is to be done by our humble ministry may be accomplished by the effect of Thy power. Through our Lord.

OMNÍPOTENS sempitérne Deus, adésto magnæ pietátis tuæ mystériis, adésto sacraméntis: et ad recreándos novos pópulos, quos tibi fons baptismátis párturit, spíritum adoptiónis emítte, ut quod nostræ humilitátis geréndum est ministério, virtútis tuæ impleátur efféctu. Per Dóminum nostrum.

℣. The Lord be with you.

℟. And with thy spirit.

℣. Lift up your hearts.

℟. We have lifted them up unto the Lord.

℣. Let us give thanks unto the Lord our God.

℟. It is meet and just.

℣. *Dóminus vobíscum.*

℟. *Et cum spíritu tuo.*

℣. *Sursum corda.*

℟. *Habémus ad Dóminum.*

℣. *Grátias agámus Dómino Deo nostro.*

℟. *Dignum et iustum est.*

VERE DIGNUM ET IUSTUM EST, æquum et salutare, nos tibi semper et ubique gratias agere, Domine, sancte Pater, omnipotens æterne Deus: qui invisibili potentia, sacramentorum tuorum mirabiliter operaris effectum: et licet nos tantis mysteriis exsequendis simus indigni: tu tamen gratiæ tuæ dona non deserens, etiam ad nostras preces aures tuæ pietatis inclinas. Deus, cuius Spiritus super aquas inter ipsa munda primordia ferebatur: ut iam tunc virtutem sanctificationis, aquarum natura conciperet. Deus, qui nocentis mundi crimina per aquas abluens, regenerationis speciem in ipsa diluvii effusione signasti: ut, unius eiusdemque elementi mysterio, et finis esset vitiis, et origo virtutibus. Respice, Domine, in faciem Ecclesiæ tuæ, et multiplica in ea regenerationes tuas, qui gratiæ tuæ affluentis impetu lætificas civitatem tuam: fontemque baptismatis aperis toto orbe terrarum gentibus innovandis: ut, tuæ maiestatis imperio, sumat Unigeniti tui gratiam de Spiritu Sancto.

IT IS TRULY MEET AND JUST, right and availing unto salvation, to give Thee thanks always and in all places, O holy Lord, almighty Father, everlasting God, Who by Thine ineffable power dost wonderfully produce the effect of Thy Sacraments: and though we are unworthy to perform such great Mysteries, yet as Thou dost not abandon the gifts of Thy grace, so Thou inclinest the ears of Thy goodness, even to our prayers. O God, Whose Spirit in the very beginning of the world moved over the waters, that even then the nature of water might receive the virtue of sanctification. O God, Who by water didst wash away the crimes of the guilty world, and by the pouring out of the deluge didst give a figure of regeneration, that one and the same element might in a mystery be the end of vice and the beginning of virtue. Look, O Lord, on the face of Thy Church, and multiply in her Thy regenerations, who by the streams of Thine abundant grace fillest Thy city with joy, and openest the font of Baptism all over the world for the renewal of the Gentiles: that by the command of Thy Majesty she may receive the grace of Thine only Son from the Holy Ghost.

With his outstretched hand, the Celebrant divides the water in the form of a cross.

QUI HANC AQUAM, *regenerandis hominibus præparatam, arcana sui numinis admixtione fecundet:*

MAY HE by a secret mixture of His divine virtue render this water fruitful for the regeneration of men, to the end that a heavenly offspring, conceived by sanctification, may emerge from the immaculate womb of this divine font, reborn a new creature: and may all, however distinguished either by sex in body, or by age in time, be brought forth to the same infancy by grace, their mother. Therefore may all unclean spirits, by Thy command, O Lord, depart far from hence: may the whole malice of diabolical deceit be entirely banished: may no power of the enemy prevail here: let him not fly about to lay his snares; may he not creep in by stealth: may he not corrupt with his poison.

ut, sanctificatione concepta, ab immaculato divini fontis utero, in novam renata creaturam, progenies cælestis emergat: et quos aut sexus in corpore, aut ætas discernit in tempore, omnes in unam pariat gratia mater infantiam. Procul ergo hinc, iubente te, Domine, omnis spiritus immundus abscedat: procul tota nequitia diabolicæ fraudis absistat. Nihil hoc loci habeat contrariæ virtutis admixtio: non insidiando cicumvolet: non latendo subrepat: non inficiendo corrumpat.

The Celebrant touches the water.

MAY THIS HOLY and innocent creature be free from all the assaults of the enemy, and purified by the destruction of all his wickedness. May it be a living fountain, a regenerating water, a purifying stream: that all those that are to be washed in this saving bath may obtain, by the operation of the Holy Ghost, the grace of a perfect cleansing.

SIT HÆC SANCTA et innocens creatura, libera ab omni impugnatoris incursu, et totius nequitiæ purgata discessu. Sit fons vivus, aqua regenerans, unda purificans: ut omnes hoc lavacro salutifero diluendi, operante in eis Spiritu Sancto, perfectæ purgationis indulgentiam consequantur.

He makes the sign of the Cross three times over the water.

THEREFORE I BLESS THEE, O creature of water, by the living ✠ God, by the true ✠ God, by the holy ✠ God: by that God Who in the beginning, separated thee by His Word from the dry land, Whose Spirit moved over thee.

UNDE BENEDICO TE, creatura aquæ, per Deum ✠ vivum, per Deum ✠ verum, per Deum ✠ sanctum: per Deum, qui te, in principio, verbo separavit ab arida: cuius Spiritus super te ferebatur.

He divides the water with his hand and throws some of it towards the four corners of the world.

QUI TE PARADISI *fonte manare fecit, et in quatuor fluminibus totam terram rigare præcepit. Qui te in deserto amaram, suavitate indita, fecit esse potabilem, et sitienti populo de petra produxit. Bene ✠ dico te et per Jesum Christum Filium eius unicum, Dominum nostrum: qui te in Cana Galilææ signo admirabili, sua potentia convertit in vinum. Qui pedibus super te ambulavit: et a Joanne in Jordane in te baptizatus est. Qui te una cum sanguine de latere suo produxit: et discipulis suis iussit, ut credentes baptizarentur in te, dicens: Ite, docete omnes gentes, baptizantes eos in nomine Patris, et Filii, et Spiritus Sancti. Hæc nobis præcepta servantibus tu, Deus omnipotens, clemens adesto: tu benignus aspira.*

WHO MADE THEE FLOW from the fountain of paradise and commanded thee to water the whole earth with thy four rivers. Who, changing thy bitterness in the desert into sweetness made thee fit to drink, and produced thee out of a rock to quench the thirsty people. I bless ✠ thee also by our Lord Jesus Christ, His only Son: Who in Cana of Galilee changed thee into wine by a wonderful miracle of His power. Who walked upon thee with dry foot, and was baptized in thee by John in the Jordan. Who made thee flow out of His side together with His Blood, and commanded His disciples that such as believed should be baptized in thee, saying: Go, teach all nations, baptizing them in the name of the Father, and of the Son, and of the Holy Ghost. Do thou, almighty God, mercifully assist us who observe this commandment: do Thou graciously inspire us.

The Celebrant breathes three times upon the water in the form of a Cross.

TU HAS SIMPLICES *aquas tuo ore benedicito: ut præter naturalem emundationem, quam lavandis possunt adhibere corporibus, sint etiam purificandis mentibus efficaces.*

DO THOU WITH THY MOUTH bless these clear waters: that besides their natural virtue of cleansing the body, they may also prove efficacious for the purifying of the soul.

He then dips the Paschal Candle in the water three times, and sings the following three times, each successively in a higher tone. As he does so he breathes upon the water in the form of the Greek letter Ψ.

MAY THE VIRTUE of the Holy Ghost descend into all the water of this font.

DESCENDAT in hanc plenitudinem fontis virtus Spiritus Sancti.

AND MAKE the whole substance of this water fruitful for regeneration.

TOTAMQUE huius aquæ substantiam, regenerandi fecundet effectu.

The Easter Candle is removed from the water.

HERE MAY the stains of all sins be washed out; here may human nature, created in Thine image, and reformed to the honor of its Author, be cleansed from all the filth of the old man: that all who receive the Sacrament of regeneration, may be born again new children of true innocence. Through our Lord Jesus Christ Thy Son: Who shall come to judge the living and the dead, and the world by fire. ℟ Amen.

HIC OMNIUM peccatorum maculæ deleantur: hic natura ad imaginem tuam condita, et ad honorem sui reformata principii, conctis vetustatis squaloribus emundetur: ut omnis homo, sacramentum hoc regenerationis ingressus, in veræ innocentiæ novam infantium renascatur. Per Dominum nostrum Jesum Christum, Filium tuum: Qui venturus est iudicare vivos et mortuos, et saeculum per ignem. ℟. Amen.

Water is reserved in the Aspersórium to be used during the Renewal of Baptismal Promises. The Celebrant pours Oil of Catechumens into the water in the form of a cross.

MAY THIS FONT BE SANCTIFIED and made fruitful by the Oil of salvation, for those who are born anew therein unto life everlasting.

SANCTIFICETUR et fecundetur fons iste Oleo salutis renascentibus ex eo, in vitam æternam.

He pours Holy Chrism into the water.

MAY THE INFUSION of the Chrism of our Lord Jesus Christ, and of the Holy Ghost the Comforter, be made in the Name of the Holy Trinity.

INFUSIO Chrismatis Domini nostri Jesu Christi, et Spiritus Sancti Paracliti, fiat in nomine santæ Trinitatis.

MAY THIS MIXTURE of the Chrism of sanctification, and of the Oil of unction, and of the water of Baptism, be made to the name of the ✠ Father, and of the ✠ Son, and of the Holy ✠ Ghost. ℟. Amen.

COMMIXTIO Chrismatis sanctificationis, et Olei unctionis, et aquæ baptismatis, pariter fiat in nomine Pa ✠ tris, et Fi ✠ lii, et Spiritus ✠ Sancti. Amen.

The vessel containing the newly blessed Baptismal Water is borne in solemn procession to the font.

ANTIPHON Psalm 41: 2-4

SICUT CERVUS *desiderat ad fontes aquarum: ita desiderat anima mea ad te, Deus. Sitivit anima mea ad Deum vivum, quando veniam, et apparebo ante faciem Dei? Fuerunt mihi lacrymæ meæ panes die ac nocte, dum dicitur mihi per singulos dies: Ubi est Deus tuus?*

AS THE HART pants after the fountains of water, so my soul pants after Thee, O God. My soul hath thirsted for the living God: when shall I come and appear before the face of God? My tears have become my bread day and night, while they say to me daily: Where is thy God?

The Baptismal Water is poured into the font and incensed.

℣. *Dóminus vobíscum.*

℣. The Lord be with you.

℟. *Et cum spíritu tuo.*

℟. And with thy spirit.

℣. *Orémus.*

℣. Let us pray.

OMNIPOTENS *sempiterne Deus, respice propitius ad devotionem populi renascentis, qui sicut cervus aquarum tuarum expetit fontem: et concede propitius, ut fidei ipsius sitis, baptismatis mysterio, animam corpusque sanctificet. Per Dominum nostrum.* ℟. *Amen.*

O ALMIGHTY and everlasting God, look mercifully on the devotion of Thy people about to be reborn, who like the hart pant after the fountain of Thy waters: and mercifully grant that the thirst of their faith may, by the Sacrament of Baptism, hallow their souls and bodies. Through our Lord. ℟. Amen.

The Baptismal Font is incensed. The Celebrant and sacred ministers return to the sanctuary.

THE RENEWAL OF BAPTISMAL PROMISES

This ceremony takes the place of the Creed as a solemn profession of our faith. The congregation holds lighted candles. Vested in a white or gold stole and cope, the Celebrant incenses the Paschal Candle.

HAC SACRATISSIMA NOCTE, *fratres carissimi, sancta Mater Ecclesia, recolens Domini nostri Jesu Christi mortem et sepulturam, eum redamando vigilat; et, celebrans eiusdem*

ON THIS MOST SACRED NIGHT, dearly beloved brethren, Holy Mother Church, recalling the death and burial of our Lord Jesus Christ, returneth His love by keeping vigil;

and aboundeth with joy at celebrating His glorious Resurrection. But because, as the Apostle teaches, we are baptized into His death and buried together with Christ: and as Christ rose again from the dead, so we too must walk in newness of life; knowing that our old man hath been crucified together with Christ so that we shall no longer be in servitude to sin. Let us look upon ourselves therefore as dead indeed to sin but living to God in Christ Jesus our Lord. Therefore, dearly beloved brethren, the Lenten observance now completed, let us renew the promises of Baptism by which formerly we renounced Satan and his works, and the world likewise, the enemy of God; and by which we promised to serve God faithfully in the Holy Catholic Church. Therefore:

gloriosam resurrectionem, laetabunda gaudet. Quoniam vero, ut docet Apostolus, consepulti sumus cum Christo per baptismum in mortem, quomodo Christus resurrexit a mortuis, ita et nos in novitate vitae oportet ambulare; scientes, veterem hominem nostrum simul cum Christo crucifixum esse, ut ultra non serviamus peccato. Existimemus ergo nos mortuos quidem esse peccato, viventes autem Deo in Christo Jesu Domino nostro. Quapropter, fratres carissimi, quadragesimali exercitatione absoluta, sancti Baptismatis promissiones renovemus, quibus olim satanae et operibus eius, sicut et mundo, qui inimicus est Dei, abrenuntiavimus, et Deo in sancta Ecclesia catholica fideliter servire promisimus. Itaque:

S. Do you renounce Satan?
℞. We do renounce him.
S. And all his works?
℞. We do renounce them.
S. And all his pomps?
℞. We do renounce them.
S. Do you believe in God the Father Almighty, Creator of heaven and earth?
℞. We do believe.
S. Do you believe in Jesus Christ, His only Son, our Lord, who was born into this world and who suffered for us?

S. *Abrenuntiatis satanae?*
℞. *Abrenuntiamus.*
S. *Et omnibus operibus eius?*
℞. *Abrenuntiamus.*
S. *Et omnibus pompis eius?*
℞. *Abrenuntiamus.*
S. *Creditis in Deum, Patrem omnipotentem, Creatorem caeli et terrae?*

℞. *Credimus.*
S. *Creditis in Jesum Christum, Filium eius unicum, Dominum nostrum, natum, et passum?*

℟. Credimus.

S. Creditis et in Spiritum Sanctum, sanctam Ecclesiam catholicam, Sanctorum communionem, remissionem peccatorum, carnis resurrectionem, et vitam aeternam?

℟. Credimus.

℟. We do believe.

S. Do you also believe in the Holy Ghost, the holy Catholic Church, the Communion of Saints, the forgiveness of sins, the resurrection of the body, and life everlasting?

℟. We do believe.

The congregation prays the Pater Noster with the Celebrant and sacred ministers. See page 23.

ET DEUS OMNIPOTENS, *Pater Domini nostri Jesu Christi, qui nos regeneravit ex aqua et Spiritu Sancto, quique nobis dedit remissionem peccatorum, ipse nos custodiat gratia sua in eodem Christo Jesu Domino nostro, in vitam aeternam. ℟. Amen.*

AND MAY GOD ALMIGHTY, the Father of our Lord Jesus Christ, Who hath regenerated us by water and the Holy Ghost, and Who hath given us remission of sins, may He by His grace keep us in the same Christ Jesus our Lord to life everlasting. ℟. Amen.

The Celebrant sprinkles the people with Baptismal Water. The candles are extinguished and the congregation kneels for the remaining litanies.

THE SECOND PART OF THE LITANIES

PROPÍTIUS ESTO, *parce nobis, Dómine.*

Propítius esto, exaudi nos, Dómine.

B E MERCIFUL, *spare us, O Lord.*
Be merciful, *graciously hear us, O Lord.*

Ab omni malo, líbera nos, Dómine.

Ab omni peccáto, *

A morte perpétua,

Per mystérium sanctæ Incarnatiónis tuæ,

Per advéntum tuum,

Per nativitátem tuum,

Per baptísmum et sanctum ieiúnium tuum,

Per crucem et passiónem tuam,

Per mortem et sepultúram tuam,

*deliver us, O Lord

From all evil, *deliver us, O Lord.*

From all sin, *

From everlasting death,

Through the mystery of Thy holy Incarnation,

Through Thy coming,

Through Thy Nativity, deliver us,

Through Thy Baptism and holy fasting,

Through Thy Cross and Passion,

Through Thy Death and Burial,

* libera nos, Domine.

Through Thy holy Resurrection,	*Per sanctam resurrectiónem tuam,*
Through Thy wonderful Ascension,	*Per admirábilem ascensiónem tuam,*
Through the coming of the Holy Ghost, the Paraclete,	*Per advéntum Spíritus Sancti Parácliti,*
In the day of judgment,	*In die iudícii,*
We sinners, we beseech Thee to hear us.	*Peccatóres, te rogámus, audi nos.*
That Thou wouldst spare us, †	*Ut nobis parcas, †*
That Thou wouldst vouchsafe to govern and preserve Thy holy Church,	*Ut Ecclésiam tuam sanctam régere et conserváre dignéris,*
That Thou wouldst vouchsafe to preserve our Apostolic Prelate, and all orders of the Church in holy religion,	*Ut domnum apostólicum et omnes ecclesiásticos órdines in sancta religióne conserváre dignéris,*
That Thou wouldst vouchsafe to humble the enemies of holy Church,	*Ut inimícos sanctæ Ecclésiæ humiliáre dignéris,*
That Thou wouldst vouchsafe to give peace and true concord to Christian kings and princes,	*Ut régibus et princípibus christiánis, pacem et veram concórdiam donáre dignéris,*
That Thou wouldst vouchsafe to confirm and preserve us in Thy holy service,	*Ut nosmetípsos in tuo sancto servítio confortáre et conserváre dignéris,*
That Thou wouldst render eternal blessings to all our benefactors,	*Ut ómnibus benefactóribus nostris sempitérna bona retríbuas,*
That Thou wouldst vouchsafe to give and preserve the fruits of the earth,	*Ut fructus terræ dare et conserváre dignéris,*
That Thou wouldst vouchsafe to grant eternal rest to all the faithful departed,	*Ut ómnibus fidélibus defúnctis réquiem ætérnam donáre dignéris,*
That Thou wouldst vouchsafe graciously to hear us,	*Ut nos exaudíre dignéris,*

* deliver us, O Lord.	* *líbera nos, Dómine.*
† we beseech Thee to hear us	† *te rogámus, audi nos.*

Agnus Dei, qui tollis peccáta mundi, parce nobis, Dómine.

Lamb of God, who takest away the sins of the world, *spare us, O Lord.*

Agnus Dei, qui tollis peccáta mundi, exaudi nos, Dómine.

Lamb of God, who takest away the sins of the world, *graciously hear us, O Lord.*

Agnus Dei, qui tollis peccáta mundi, miserére nobis.

Lamb of God, who takest away the sins of the world, *have mercy on us.*

Christe, audi nos.

Christ, hear us.

Christe, exáudi nos.

Christ, graciously hear us.

≈ Mass ≈

The prayers at the foot of the Altar are omitted, and bells are rung during the Gloria as the church is brightly lit to celebrate the resurrection of Christ.

COLLECT

DEUS, qui hanc sacratíssimum noctem gloria domínicæ Resurrectiónis illústras: consérva in nova famíliæ tuæ progénie adoptiónis spíritum, quem dedísti, ut córpore et mente renováti puram tibi exhíbeant servitútem. Per eundem Dominum nostrum.

O GOD, Who dost illuminate this most holy night by the glory of the Lord's Resurrection, preserve in the new children of Thy family the spirit of adoption which Thou hast given; that renewed in body and mind, they may render to Thee a pure service. Through the same our Lord.

EPISTLE *Colossians 3: 1-4*

FRATRES: Si consurrexistis cum Christo, quae sursum sunt quaerite, ubi Christus est in dextera Dei sedens: quae sursum sunt sapite, non quae super terram. Mortui enim estis, et vita vestra est abscondita cum Christo in Deo. Cum Christus apparuerit, vita vestra: tunc et vos apparebitis cum ipso in gloria.

BRETHREN, if you be risen with Christ, seek the things that are above, where Christ is sitting at the right hand of God: mind the things that are above, not the things that are upon the earth. For you are dead, and your life is hidden with Christ in God. When Christ shall appear, Who is your life, then you also shall appear with Him in glory.

STAND *for the Solemn Alleluia.*

ALLELUIA *Psalm 117: 1*

ALLELUIA. Give praise to the Lord for He is good: for His mercy endureth forever.

ALLELUIA. *Confitemini Domino, quoniam bonus: quoniam in saeculum misericordia eius.*

TRACT *Psalm 116: 1, 2*

O PRAISE THE LORD, all ye nations, and praise Him, all ye people. For His mercy is confirmed upon us: and the truth of the Lord remaineth forever.

LAUDATE DOMINUM, *omnes gentes: et collaudate eum, omnes populi. Quoniam confirmata est super nos misericordia eius: et veritas Domini manet in aeternum.*

GOSPEL *Matthew 28: 1-7*

AND IN THE END of the Sabbath, when it began to dawn towards the first day of the week, came Mary Magdalen and the other Mary to see the sepulcher. And behold there was a great earthquake. For an Angel of the Lord descended from heaven, and coming, rolled back the stone and sat upon it: and his countenance was as lightening and his raiment as snow. And for fear of him the guards were struck with terror and became as dead men. And the Angel answering, said to the women: Fear ye not: for I know that you seek Jesus who was crucified: He is not here: for He is risen, as He said. Come and see the place where the Lord was laid. And going quickly, tell ye His disciples that He is risen: and behold He will go before you into Galilee: there you shall see Him. Lo, I have foretold it to you.

VESPERE *autem sabbati, quae lucescit in prima sabbati, venit Maria Magdalene, et altera Maria videre sepulcrum. Et ecce terraemotus factus est magnus. Angelus enim Domini descendit de caelo: et accedens revolvit lapidem, et sedebat super eum: erat autem aspectus eius sicut fulgur: et vestimentum eius sicut nix. Prae timore autem eius exterriti sunt custodes, et facti sunt velut mortui. Respondens autem Angelus, dixit mulieribus: Nolite timere vos: scio enim, quod Jesum, qui crucifixus est, quaeritis: non est hic: surrexit enim, sicut dixit. Venite, et videte locum, ubi positus erat Dominus. Et cito euntes, dicite discipulis eius, quia surrexit: et ecce praecedit vos in Galilaeam: ibi eum videbitis. Ecce praedixi vobis.*

The Offertory antiphon is omitted.

SECRET

SUSCIPE, quaesumus, Domine, preces populi tui, cum oblationibus hostiarum: ut paschalibus initiata mysteriis, ad aeternitatis nobis medelam, te operante, proficiant. Per Dominum nostrum.

ACCEPT, we beseech Thee, O Lord, the prayers of Thy people together with the sacrifice they offer: that what has been begun by the Paschal Mysteries, may by Thine arrangement result in our eternal healing. Through our Lord.

PREFACE OF EASTER

VERE DIGNUM ET IUSTUM EST, æquum et salutare, te quidem Domine omni tempore, sed in hoc potissimum nocte gloriosis prædicare, cum Pascha nostrum immolatus est Christus. Ipse enim verus est Angus qui abstulit peccáta mundi. Qui mortem nostram moriendo destruxit, et vitam resurgendo reparavit. Et ideo cum Angelis et Archangelis, cum Thronis et Dominationibus, cumque omnia milita coelestis exercitus, hymnum gloriæ tuæ canimus, sine fine dicentes...

IT IS TRULY MEET AND JUST, right and for our salvation, at all times to praise Thee, O Lord, but more gloriously especially on this night, when Christ our Pasch was sacrificed. For He is the true Lamb who hath taken away the sins of the world. Who by dying hath destroyed our death, and by rising again hath restored us to life. And therefore with Angels and Archangels, with Thrones and Dominions, and with all the hosts of the heavenly army, we sing the hymn of Thy glory, ever more saying...

THE SOLEMN LAUDS OF EASTER DAY
Lauds takes the place of the Communion antiphon.

ANTIPHON *Psalm 150*

ALLELUIA, ALLELUIA, ALLELUIA. Laudáte Dóminum in sanctis eius, laudáte eum in firmaménto virtútis eius.

ALLELUIA, ALLELUIA, ALLELUIA. Praise ye the Lord in His holy places: praise ye Him in the firmament of His power.

Laudáte eum in virtútibus eius, laudáte eum secúndum multitúdinem magnitúdinis eius.

Praise ye Him for His mighty acts: praise ye Him according to the multitude of His greatness.

Praise Him with sound of trumpets: praise Him with psaltery and harp.

Laudáte eum in sono tubæ, laudáte eum in psaltério, et cíthara.

Praise Him with timbrel and choir: praise Him with strings and organs.

Laudáte eum in týmpano, et choro: laudáte eum in chordis et órgano.

Praise Him on high sounding cymbals: praise Him on cymbals of joy. Let every spirit praise the Lord.

Laudáte eum in cýmbalis benesonántibus: laudáte eum in cýmbalis iubilatiónis: omnes spíritus laudet Dóminum.

℣. Glory be to the Father, and to the Son, and to the Holy Ghost.

℞. As it was in the beginning, is now, and ever shall be, world without end. Amen. Alleluia, alleluia, alleluia.

℣. Glória Patri, et Fílio, et Spirítui Sancto.

℞. Sicut erat in princípio, et nunc, et semper, et in sǽcula sæculórum. Amen. Allelúia, allelúia, allelúia.

ANTIPHON And very early in the morning, the first day of the week, they came to the sepulcher, the sun being now risen, alleluia.

Et valde mane una sabbatórum, véniunt ad monuméntum, orto iam sole, allelúia.

The altar is incensed during the singing of the Benedictus.

BLESSED BE ✠ THE LORD GOD of Israel; because He hath visited and wrought the redemption of His people: And hath raised up an horn of salvation to us, in the house of David His servant, As He spoke by the mouth of His holy prophets, who are from the beginning, Salvation from our enemies, and from the hand of all that hate us: To perform mercy to our fathers, and to remember His holy testament, The oath, which He swore to Abraham our father, that He would grant to us, That being delivered from the hand of our enemies, we may

BENEDICTUS ✠ DÓMINUS DEUS Israël: quia visitávit et fecit redemptiónem plebis suæ: Et eréxit cornu salútis nobis: in domo David, púeri sui. Sicut locútus est per os sanctórum, qui a sæculo sunt, prophetárum ejus: Salútem ex inimícis nostris et de manu ómnium qui odérunt nos. Ad faciéndam misericórdiam cum pátribus nostris: et memorári testaménti sui sancti. Jusjurándum, quod jurávit ad Abraham patrem nostrum, datúrum se nobis: Ut sine timóre, de manu inimicórum nostrórum liberáti, serviámus illi. In sanctitáte et justítia coram ipso, ómnibus diébus nostris. Et tu, puer, Prophéta Altíssimi vocáberis: præíbis enim ante fáciem Dómini, paráre vias ejus: Ad dandam sciéntiam salútis plebi ejus, in remissiónem peccatórum eórum: Per víscera misericórdiæ Dei nostri: in quibus visitávit nos, óriens ex alto: Illumináre his, qui in ténebris et in umbra mortis sedent: ad dirigéndos pedes nostros in viam pacis. Glória Patri, et Fílio, et Spirítui Sancto. Sicut erat in princípio, et nunc, et semper, et in sæcula sæculórum. Amen.

serve Him without fear, In holiness and justice before Him, all our days. And thou, child, shalt be called the prophet of the Highest, for thou shalt go before the face of the Lord to prepare His ways: To give knowledge of salvation to His people, unto the remission of their sins: Through the bowels of the mercy of our God, in which the Orient from on high hath visited us: To enlighten them that sit in darkness, and in the shadow of death: to direct our feet into the way of peace. Glory be to the Father, and to the Son, and to the Holy Ghost. As it was in the beginning, is now, and ever shall be, world without end. Amen.

Et valde mane una sabbatórum, véniunt ad monuméntum, orto iam sole, allelúia.

ANT. And very early in the morning, the first day of the week, they came to the sepulcher, the sun being now risen, alleluia.

POSTCOMMUNION

SPÍRITUM NOBIS, Dómine, tuæ caritátis infúnde: ut, quos sacraméntis Paschálibus satiásti tua fácias pietáte concórdes. Per Dominum nostrum.

POUR FORTH UPON US, O Lord, the spirit of Thy love: that those whose hunger Thou hast satisfied with the Sacraments of Easter may in Thy kindness be one in heart. Through our Lord.

White   # EASTER SUNDAY   *First Class*

SOLEMN EASTER PROCESSION

℣. Let us go forth in peace.   ℟. *Procedamus in pace.*

During the solemn procession the following hymn is sung.

SALVE FESTA

℟. HAIL, FESTAL DAY, hallowed forever, on which God defeats hell and seizes Heaven.

℣. LO! OUR EARTH is in her spring, bearing thus her witness that, with her Lord, she has all her gifts restored. ℟. Hail, festal day...

℣. For now the woods with their leaves and the meadows with their flowers, pay homage to Jesus' triumph over the gloomy tomb. ℟. Hail, festal day...

℣. Light, firmament, fields and sea, give justly praise to the God that defeats the laws of death, and rises above the stars. ℟. Hail, festal day...

℣. The crucified God now reigns over all things; and every creature to its Creator tells a prayer. ℟. Hail, festal day...

℣. O Jesus! Savior of the world! Loving Creator and Redeemer! Only-begotten Son of God the Father! ℟. Hail, festal day...

℣. Seeing the human race was sunk in misery deep, Thou wast made Man, that Thou might rescue man. ℟. Hail, festal day...

℟. *SALVE, FESTA DIES, toto venerabilis aevo, qua deus infernum vicit et astra tenet.*

℣. *ECCE RENASCENTIS testatur gratia mundi omnia cum domino dona redisse suo.* ℟. *Salve, festa dies...*

℣. *Namque triumphanti post tristia Tartara Christo undique fronde nemus, gramina flore favent.* ℟. *Salve, festa dies...*

℣. *Legibus inferni oppressis super astra meantem laudant rite deum lux polus arva fretum.* ℟. *Salve, festa dies...*

℣. *Qui crucifixus erat, deus ecce per omnia regnat, dantque creatori cuncta creata precem.* ℟. *Salve, festa dies...*

℣. *Christe salus rerum, bone conditor atque redemptor, unica progenies ex deitate patris.* ℟. *Salve, festa dies...*

℣. *Qui genus humanum cernens mersisse profundo, ut hominem eriperes es quoque factus homo.* ℟. *Salve, festa dies...*

⁓ Mass ⁓

INTROIT *Psalm 138: 18, 5, 6, 1-2*

RESURRÉXI, *et adhuc tecum sum, allelúia: posuísti super me manum tuam, allelúia: mirábilis facta est sciéntia tua, allelúia, allelúia. Dómine, probásti me, et cognovísti me: tu cognovísti sessiónem meam, et resurrectiónem meam. Glória Patri. Resurréxi, et adhuc tecum sum, allelúia.*

I AROSE and am still with thee, alleluia: Thou hast laid Thine hand upon me, alleluia: Thy knowledge is become wonderful, alleluia, alleluia. Lord, Thou has searched me and known me: Thou knowest my sitting down and my rising up. Glory be to the Father. I arose and am still with thee, alleluia.

COLLECT

DEUS, *qui hodiérna die per Unigénitum tuum, æternitátis nobis áditum devícta morte reserásti: vota nostra, quæ prævueniéndo aspíras, étiam adjuvándo proséquere. Per eúmdem Dóminum.*

O GOD, Who on this day through Thine only-begotten Son hast overcome death and opened unto us the gate of everlasting life, do Thou follow with Thine aid the desires which Thou dost put into our minds, and by Thy continual help bring the same to good effect. Through the same Lord.

EPISTLE *I Corinthians 5: 7, 8*

FRATRES: *Expurgáte vetus ferméntum, ut sitis nova conspérsio, sicut estis ázymi. Étenim Pascha nostrum immolátus est Christus. Ítaque epulémur, non in ferménto véteri, neque in ferménto malítiæ et nequítiæ: sed in ázymis sinceritátis et veritátis.*

BRETHREN, purge out the old leaven, that you may be a new paste, as you are unleavened: for Christ our Pasch is sacrificed. Therefore let us feast, not with the old leaven, nor with the leaven of malice and wickedness, but with the unleavened bread of sincerity and truth.

GRADUAL *Psalm 117: 24, 1*

HÆC DIES *quam fecit Dóminus: exsultémus et lætémur in ea. Confitémini Dómino, quóniam bonus: quóniam in saéculum misericórida ejus.*

THIS IS THE DAY which the Lord hath made: let us rejoice and be glad in it. Give praise unto the Lord, for He is good: for His mercy endureth for ever.

ALLELUIA *I Corinthians 5: 7*

ALLELUIA, ALLELUIA. Christ our Pasch is sacrificed.

ALLELÚIA, ALLELÚIA. Pascha nostrum immolátus est Christus.

EASTER SEQUENCE *For chant see page 130*

CHRISTIANS! To the Paschal Victim offer your thankful praises. The Lamb the sheep redeemeth: Christ, Who only is sinless, reconcileth sinners to the Father. Death and life contended in that conflict stupendous: the Prince of Life, Who died, deathless reigneth. Speak, Mary, declaring what thou sawest wayfaring: The tomb of Christ Who now liveth: and likewise the glory of the Risen. Bright angels attesting, the shroud and napkin resting. Yea, Christ my Hope is arisen: to Galilee He goeth before you. We know that Christ is risen, henceforth ever-living: Have mercy, Victor King, pardon-giving. Amen. Alleluia.

VÍCTIMÆ PASCHÁLI laudes ímmo-lent Christiáni. Agnus redémit oves: Christus ínnocens Patri reconciliávit peccatóres. Mors et vita duéllo conf-lixére mirándo: dux vitæ mórtuus, regnat vivus. Dic nobis, María, quid vidísti in via? Sepúlchrum Christi vivéntis: et glóriam vidi resurgéntis. Angélicos testes, sudárium, et vestes. Surréxit Christus spes mea: præcédet vos in Galilaéam. Scimus Christum surrexísse a mórtuis vere: Tu nobis, victor Rex, miserére. Amen. Allelúia.

GOSPEL *Mark 16: 1-7*

AT THAT TIME, Mary Magdalen and Mary, the mother of James, and Salome bought sweet spices, that coming they might anoint Jesus. And very early in the morning, the first day of the week, they came to the sepulcher, the sun being now risen. And they said one to another: Who shall roll back for us the stone from the door of the sepulcher? And looking, they saw the stone rolled back, for it was very great. And entering into the sepulcher, they saw a young man sitting

IN ILLO TÉMPORE: María Magdaléne, et María Jacóbi, et Salóme emérunt arómata, ut veniéntes úngerent Jesum. Et valde mane una sabbatórum, véniunt ad monuméntum, orto jam sole. Et dicébant ad ínvicem: Quis revólvet nobis lápidem ab óstio monuménti? Et respiciéntes, vidérunt revolútum lápidem. Erat quippe magnus valde. Et introëúntes in monuméntum vidérunt júvenem sedéntem in dextris, coopértum stola cándida, et obstupuérunt. Qui dicit illis: Nolíte expavéscere: Jesum quaéritis Nazarénum, crucifíxum: surréxit, non est hic, ecce locus ubi posuérunt eum. Sed ite, dícite discípulis ejus, et Petro, quia præcédit vos in Galilaéam: ibi eum vidébitis, sicut dixit vobis.

on the right side, clothed with a white robe, and they were astonished. Who saith to them: Be not afraid; ye seek Jesus of Nazareth, Who was crucified: He is risen, He is not here; behold the place where they laid Him. But go, tell His disciples, and Peter, that He goeth before you into Galilee: there you shall see Him, as He told you.

OFFERTORY *Psalm 75: 9, 10*

TERRA TRÉMUIT, et quiévit, dum resúrgeret in iudício Deus, allelúia.

THE EARTH TREMBLED and was still when God arose in judgment, alleluia.

SECRET

SÚSCIPE, quaésumus, Dómine, preces pópuli tui cum oblatiónibus hostiárum: ut paschálibus initiáta mystériis, ad æternitátis nobis medélam, te operánte, profíciant. Per Dóminum nostrum.

ACCEPT, we beseech Thee, O Lord, the prayers of Thy people with the oblation of sacrifice, that what we have begun by these Paschal mysteries, may by Thy operation, profit us for a healing remedy unto everlasting life. Through our Lord.

PREFACE OF EASTER

VERE DIGNUM ET IUSTUM EST, æquum et salutare, te quidem Domine omni tempore, sed in hoc potissimum nocte gloriosis prædicare, cum Pascha nostrum immolatus est Christus. Ipse enim verus est Angus qui abstulit peccáta mundi. Qui mortem nostram moriendo destruxit, et vitam resurgendo reparavit. Et ideo cum Angelis et Archangelis, cum Thronis et Dominationibus, cumque omnia milita coelestis exercitus,

IT IS TRULY MEET AND JUST, right and for our salvation, at all times to praise Thee, O Lord, but more gloriously especially on this night, when Christ our Pasch was sacrificed. For He is the true Lamb Who hath taken away the sins of the world. Who by dying hath destroyed our death, and by rising again hath restored us to life. And therefore with Angels and Archangels, with Thrones and Dominions, and with all the hosts of the heavenly army, we sing the hymn of Thy glory, ever more saying...

hymnum gloriæ tuæ canimus, sine fine dicentes...

COMMUNION *I Corinthians 5: 7, 8*

CHRIST OUR PASCH is immolated, alleluia: therefore let us feast with the unleavened bread of sincerity and truth, alleluia, alleluia, alleluia.

PASCHA NOSTRUM immolátus est Christus, allelúia: ítaque epulémur in ázymis sinceritátis et veritátis, allelúia, allelúia, allelúia.

HYMN O FILII ET FILIAE *see page 131*

POSTCOMMUNION

POUR FORTH UPON US, O Lord, the Spirit of Thy love, that by Thy loving kindness Thou may make of one mind those whom Thou hast fed with these Paschal sacraments. Through our Lord.

SPÍRITUM NOBIS, Dómine, tuæ caritátis infúnde: ut, quos sacraméntis Paschálibus satiásti, tua fácias pietáte concórdes. Per Dóminum nostrum.

God in the Night

BY FATHER ABRAM J. RYAN

Deep in the dark I hear the feet of God
He walks in the world; He puts His holy hand
On every sleeper—only puts His hand—
Within it benedictions for each one—
Then passes on; but ah! whene'er He meets
A watcher waiting for Him, He is glad.
(Does God, like man, feel lonely in the dark?)
He rests His hand upon the watcher's brow—
But more than that, He leaves His very breath
Upon the watcher's soul; and more than this,
He stays for holy hours where watchers pray;
And more than that, He ofttimes lifts the veils
That hide the visions of the world unseen.
The brightest sanctities of highest souls
Have blossomed into beauty in the dark.
How extremes meet! The very darkest crimes
That blight the souls of men are strangely born
Beneath the shadows of the holy night. ✠

EXCERPTED FROM THE LONGER POEM OF THIS TITLE.

CHANTS FOR THE SEASON

PANGE LINGUA

III

Pange língua glori-ósi Córporis Mystéri-um,

Sanguínisque pre-ti-ósi, Quem in múndi pré-ti-um

Frúctus véntris generósi Rex effúdit génti-um.

2. Nóbis dá-tus, nóbis nátus Ex Intácta Vírgine,

Et in múndo conversátus, Spárso vérbi sémine,

Sú-i móras incolátus Miro clausit órdine 3. In

suprémae nócte coénae Recúmbens cum frátribus,

Observáta lége plene Cíbis in legá-libus, Cíbum

túrbae du-odénae Se dat sú-is mánibus. 4. Vérbum

cáro, pánem vérum Vérbo cárnem éfficit: Fítque

sánguis Chrísti mérum, Et si sénsus dé-fi-cit,

Ad firmándum cor sincérum Sóla fídes súfficit. *

5. Tántum ergo Sacraméntum Venerémur cérnu-i:

Et antíquum documéntum Nóvo cédat rítu- i:

Praestet fídes supplémentum Sénsu-um de-féctu-i.

6. Genitó-ri, Genitóque Laus et jubi-lá-ti-o, Sálus,

honor, vírtus quoque Sit et benedictí- o: Procéd-

enti ab utróque Cómpar sit laudá-ti-o. Amen.

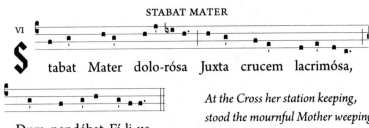

STABAT MATER

tabat Mater dolo-rósa Juxta crucem lacrimósa,

Dum pendébat Fí-li-us.

At the Cross her station keeping,
stood the mournful Mother weeping,
close to her Son to the last.

Cuius animam gementem,
Contristatam et dolentem
Pertransivit gladius.

Through her heart, His sorrow sharing,
All His bitter anguish bearing,
Now at length the sword has passed.

O quam tristis et afflicta
Fuit illa benedicta,
Mater Unigeniti!

O how sad and sore distressed
Was that Mother, highly blest,
Of the Sole-begotten One.

Quae maerebat et dolebat,
Pia Mater, dum videbat
Nati poenas inclyti.

Christ above in torment hangs,
She beneath beholds the pangs
Of her dying glorious Son.

Quis est homo qui non fleret,
Matrem Christi si videret
In tanto supplicio?

Is there one who would not weep,
Whelmed in miseries so deep,
Christ's dear Mother to behold?

Quis non posset contristari
Christi Matrem contemplari
Dolentem cum Filio?

Can the human heart refrain
From partaking in her pain,
In that Mother's pain untold?

Pro peccatis suae gentis
Vidit Iesum in tormentis,
Et flagellis subditum.

Bruised, derided, cursed, defiled,
She beheld her tender Child
All with bloody scourges rent.

Vidit suum dulcem Natum
Moriendo desolatum,
Dum emisit spiritum.

For the sins of His own nation,
Saw Him hang in desolation,
Till His spirit forth He sent.

O thou Mother! Fount of love!
Touch my spirit from above,
Make my heart with thine accord.

Make me feel as thou hast felt;
Make my soul to glow and melt
With the love of Christ my Lord.

Holy Mother! Pierce me through,
In my heart each wound renew
Of my Savior crucified:

Let me share with thee His pain,
Who for all my sins was slain,
Who for me in torments died.

Let me mingle tears with thee,
Mourning Him who mourned for me,
All the days that I may live:

By the Cross with thee to stay,
There with thee to weep and pray,
Is all I ask of thee to give.

Virgin of all virgins blest!,
Listen to my fond request:
Let me share thy grief divine;

Let me, to my latest breath,
In my body bear the death
Of that dying Son of thine.

Wounded with His every wound,
Steep my soul till it hath swooned,
In His very Blood away;

Be to me, O Virgin, nigh,
Lest in flames I burn and die,
In His awful Judgment Day.

Eia, Mater, fons amoris
Me sentire vim doloris
Fac, ut tecum lugeam.

Fac, ut ardeat cor meum
In amando Christum Deum
Ut sibi complaceam.

Sancta Mater, istud agas,
Crucifixi fige plagas
Cordi meo valide.

Tui Nati vulnerati,
Tam dignati pro me pati,
Poenas mecum divide.

Fac me tecum pie flere,
Crucifixo condolere,
Donec ego vixero.

Iuxta Crucem tecum stare,
Et me tibi sociare
In planctu desidero.

Virgo virginum praeclara,
Mihi iam non sis amara,
Fac me tecum plangere.

Fac, ut portem Christi mortem,
Passionis fac consortem,
Et plagas recolere.

Fac me plagis vulnerari,
Fac me Cruce inebriari,
Et cruore Filii.

Flammis ne urar succensus,
Per te, Virgo, sim defensus
In die iudicii.

Christe, cum sit hinc exire,
Da per Matrem me venire
Ad palmam victoriae.

Quando corpus morietur,
Fac, ut animae donetur
Paradisi gloria. Amen.

Christ, when Thou shalt call me hence,
By Thy Mother my defense,
By Thy Cross my victory;

While my body here decays,
May my soul Thy goodness praise,
Safe in paradise with Thee. Amen.

EASTER SEQUENCE

ictimæ paschá-li láudes * ímmolent Christi-áni

Agnus redémit óves: Chrístus ínnocens Pátri

reconci-li-ávit peccatóres. Mors et ví-ta du-éllo conflixére

mirándo: dux vítæ mórtu-us, régnat vívus. Dic nóbis

Marí-a, quid vidísti in ví-a? Sepúlcrum Chrísti vivéntis,

et glóri-am vídi resurgéntis Angé-licos téstes, sudári-um,

et véstes. Surréxit Chrístus spes mé-a: præcédet sú-os

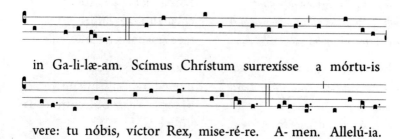

in Ga-li-læ-am. Scímus Chrístum surrexísse   a mórtu-is

vere: tu nóbis, víctor Rex, mise-ré-re.   A- men.   Allelú-ia.

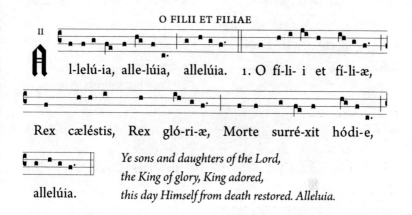

O FILII ET FILIAE

l-lelú-ia, alle-lúia,   allelúia.   1. O fí-li- i et fí-li-æ,

Rex cæléstis, Rex gló-ri-æ, Morte surré-xit hódi-e,

allelúia.

Ye sons and daughters of the Lord,
the King of glory, King adored,
this day Himself from death restored. Alleluia.

All in the early morning gray
went holy women on their way,
to see the tomb where Jesus lay.
Alleluia.

Ex mane prima Sabbati
ad ostium monumenti
accesserunt discipuli. Alleluia.

Of spices pure a precious store
in their pure hands these women bore,
to anoint the sacred Body o'er. Alleluia.

Et Maria Magdalene,
et Iacobi, et Salome
Venerunt corpus ungere. Alleluia.

Then straightaway one in white
they see,
who saith, "Seek the Lord: but He
is risen and gone to Galilee." Alleluia.

In albis sedens angelus
praedixit mulieribus:
In Galilaea est Dominus. Alleluia.

This told they Peter, told John;
who forthwith to the tomb are gone,
but Peter is by John outrun. Alleluia.

Et Ioannes apostolus
cucurrit Petro citius,
monumento venit prius. Alleluia.

That self-same night, while out of fear
the doors where shut, their Lord
  most dear
to His Apostles did appear. Alleluia.

Discipulis astantibus,
in medio stetit Christus,
dicens: Pax vobis omnibus.
  Alleluia.

But Thomas, when of this he heard,
was doubtful of his brethren's word;
wherefore again there comes the Lord.
  Alleluia.

Ut intellexit Didymus
quia surrexerat Iesus,
remansit fere dubius. Alleluia.

"Thomas, behold my side," saith He;
"My hands, My feet, My body see,
and doubt not, but believe in Me."
  Alleluia.

Vide Thoma, vide latus,
vide pedes, vide manus,
noli esse incredulus. Alleluia.

When Thomas saw that wounded side,
The truth no longer he denied;
"Thou art my Lord and God!" he
  cried. Alleluia!

Quando Thomas Christi latus,
Pedes vidit atque manus,
Dixit: Tu es Deus meus. Alleluia!

Oh, blest are they who have not seen
Their Lord and yet believe in Him!
Eternal life awaiteth them. Alleluia!

Beati qui non viderunt,
Et firmiter crediderunt
Vitam aeternam habebunt.
  Alleluia!

Now let us praise the Lord most high,
And strive His name to magnify
On this great day, through earth and
  sky: Alleluia.

In hoc festo sanctissimo
Sit laus et jubilatio,
Benedicamus Domino. Alleluia!

Whose mercy ever runneth o'er;
Whom men and Angel hosts adore;
To Him be glory evermore. Alleluia!

Ex quibus nos humillimas
Devotas atque debitas
Deo dicamus gratias. Alleluia!

CPSIA information can be obtained at www.ICGtesting.com
Printed in the USA
BVOW05s1750230314

348507BV00006B/118/P